Gabriel Bonvalot, C. B. Pitman

Across Tibet being a translation of: 'De Paris au Tonkin à travers le Tibet inconnu'

Vol II

Gabriel Bonvalot, C. B. Pitman

Across Tibet being a translation of: 'De Paris au Tonkin à travers le Tibet inconnu'
Vol II

ISBN/EAN: 9783742870490

Manufactured in Europe, USA, Canada, Australia, Japa

Cover: Foto ©Andreas Hilbeck / pixelio.de

Manufactured and distributed by brebook publishing software (www.brebook.com)

Gabriel Bonvalot, C. B. Pitman

Across Tibet being a translation of: 'De Paris au Tonkin à travers le Tibet inconnu'

ACROSS THIBET.

BEING A TRANSLATION OF

"DE PARIS AU TONKIN À TRAVERS LE TIBET INCONNU,"

BY

GABRIEL BONVALOT.

With Illustrations from Photographs taken by Prince Henry of Orleans, and Map of Route.

TRANSLATED BY C. B. PITMAN.

Vol. II.

CASSELL & COMPANY, Limited:
LONDON, PARIS & MELBOURNE.

CONTENTS OF VOL. II.

CHAPTER IX.
AMONG THE THIBETANS.

"A Man is Coming"—Description of the First Thibetan Encountered—Thibetan Horsemen—Driving a Bargain—A Savage's First Sight of a Watch—Uncomplimentary Comments—On the High Road to Lhassa—Getting Information under Difficulties—English and Russians in Bad Odour—Lake Burben-cho—The Dungan shows his Seals—Silos—A Thibetan Interior—A Native Woman—Imatch Done up—Prayers Engraved on Stones—Taking a Prisoner—Death of Imatch—In Sight of the Ningling Tangla and the Namtso ... ... 1—33

CHAPTER X.
AWAITING ORDERS FROM LHASSA.

At Namtso—Encamping near Ningling Tangla Pass—An Embassage—The Thibetans Undecided—The Caravan in Battle Array—A Mandarin—A Mongolian Interpreter—Arrival of the Amban from Lhassa—Giving him Audience—His Suite and their Costumes—A Long Interview—The Thibetans' New Year's Day—In the Amban's Tent—Gibeonites—Another Mongolian Interpreter—The Apathy of Thibetans—A Storm—Arrival of the Ta-Lama and the Ta-Amban—Plain Speaking—Refusal to Return—The Ta-Lama and the Ta-Amban described—Abdullah and the Dungan at their Devotions—Colloquy between Rachmed and Timour—Thibetans at Work—Their General Characteristics—Carnivorous Horses—The Samda Kansain Mountains—The Samda Tchou River—A Blade of Grass—How they do Business at Lhassa ... ... 34—70

CHAPTER XI.
PRESENTS FROM LHASSA.

Breakfasting with the Ta-Amban and Ta-Lama—Diplomatic Indignation—Two Barbarian Petty Chiefs—An Effectual Call to Order—A Sunset Scene—Feasting on a Sheep's Head—A "Dainty Dish"—At Soubron—Resting at Di-Ti—Water-Carriers—An *Entente Cordiale*—Characteristics and Habits of the Natives of the Di-Ti Country—A Specimen of Primeval Man—Nigan: Another Stoppage—The Takai-Lama's Presents: Sacred Objects—Return Presents—A Lama Guide—The Ta-Amban's Advice—A Pet Ram—Timour, Parpa, and Iça Go Back ... ... 71—91

CHAPTER XII.
SO AND ITS LAMA-HOUSE.

At Gatine—The River Ourtchou—A Hermit Lama—"Steeped in Luxury"—At Djaucounnene—Meeting a Caravan—Resemblance between Thibetans and other Peoples—Thumb Language—A Droll Native—The Thibetans not Fanatics—On the Banks of the Omtchou—At Tandi—The Thibetan Sling—A Superb Mountain Scene—A Sight of Ploughed Land—First View of the Lama-house of So—The "Delicious Odour" of Wood—A *Concierge* in Thibet—Native Money—A Commission of 150 per Cent.—Ploughing at So—Crossing the Sotchou—A Bearded Thibetan—Why Dishonest Chiefs are Popular ... ... 92—119

CHAPTER XIII.
NATIVE CUSTOMS AND CHARACTERS.

A Thibetan Vitellius—*Chang*—Commercial Chinamen—Native Women—Polyandry and Polygamy—Beggars—Contentment—The Chief of the District at Home—A Theological Question—Departure from Sérésumdo—Mendicant Lamas and their Music—News from Lhassa—The Honeymoon in Thibet—Novel Method of Crossing a Stream—Tumblers—A Chief in his Cups—A Scene of Home Life—*Force Majeure*—Fickleness of the Natives: the Probable Cause—At Karimeta—Primitive Husbandry—A Lamaess—Praying Windmills—Tchoungo—The Däla and Djala Passes—A Splendid Prospect—A Pagoda—Houmda—Lagoun: a Manufacturing Town ... ... 120—151

CHAPTER XIV.
FROM LAGOUN TO CHANGKA.

Lamé—Lamda—Bad Food—Religious Malthusianism—Crossing the Satchou—Capture of a New-born Monkey—Koushoune—Ouoshishoune—A Fat Lama—Dzérine—Hassar—Thibetans and Chinese: a Contrast—Indefinite Dates—Rough and Ready Justice—Dotou—A Dignified Chinese Official—A Series of Prayer Mills—Rachmed in Action—The Chinese Army—Parting with the Lama Guide—Tsonké—A Secret Christian—The Destruction of the Batang Mission—Burial-place of a French Missionary—Reception by the Mandarin of Changka—Four Swords for 150 Men... 152—181

CHAPTER XV.
BATANG, TATSIEN-LOU, AND TONQUIN.

Religious Prophylactics—"Red" and "Yellow" Lamaism—The Lamas as Capitalists—From Changka to Konshou—The Tea Trade between China and Thibet—Leindünne—Anarchy—Chinese Inns—The Blue River (Kin-sha-Kiang)—Frenchmen in Thibet—Chinese Justice—An Orgie—Chinese Soldiers: the Courage of Numbers—At Batang—A Series of Questions—Tatsien-Lou—The French Missionaries There—A Difficulty with the Mandarin—Apology—Chinese Administration—Sending Home the Photographs—The Red River—On French Soil—Hanoï—The Future of Tonquin—Conclusion ... ... 182—221

LIST OF ILLUSTRATIONS IN VOL. II.

	PAGE
Talking Over the First Thibetans	9
Tent at Burben-cho	16
Thibetans at Burben-cho	17
Thibetan Horsemen	21
A Petty Chief	25
The Namtso	29
Pack-Horses	33
Religious Insignia	34
The Petty Amban	41
Tent of the Envoys from Lhassa	48
Thibetans Loading a Yak	56
The Caravan in Motion	65
The Cooking Tent	70
Chief of the Djashas	71
Thibetan Savages round a Fire	76
The Ta-Lama, the Ta-Amban, and other Chiefs from Lhassa	81
A Thibetan Saluting	85
The Lama Guide	88
An Attendant of the Amban	89
Thibetan Horsemen	91
Monument near the Lama-house of So	92
Thibetan of the Redskin Type	97
Yak Driver with Prayer-mill	100
A Loaded Yak	104
The Lama-house at So	109
A House at So	113
Women at Bata-Soumdo	119
Woman and Child of Sérésumdo	120
House at Sérésumdo	121
Types of Natives at Sérésumdo	125
Mendicant Lamas	129
Scene near Sérésumdo	137
The "Obo" at Tchoungo	145
Prayers Carved on a Stone	151

TIBETAN OF TIÉCHOUNG...	152
A TIBETAN VILLAGE	153
BRIDGE AT SOUGOMBA	157
CROSSING THE SATCHOU ...	161
GROUP OF NATIVES	168
SCENE IN INHABITED THIBET	169
RUINS IN THE MAKTCHOU VALLEY	176
LAMA-HOUSE AT DOTOU	177
PRAYER-MILL AT DOTOU	181
A DANCER	182
DANCERS AT CHANGKA	185
A BUDDHIST CHAPEL	187
THE KIN-SHA-KIANG (GREAT BLUE RIVER)	189
WOMEN AT BATANG	192
LAMAS AT BATANG	193
GENERAL VIEW OF LITANG	197
LITANG: VIEW FROM THE ROOFS	200
CHINESE FORT AT LITANG	201
ENTRANCE TO THE TATSIEN-LOU VALLEY	204
FRENCH MISSIONARIES	208
FISHING WITH CORMORANTS	212
LOLOS	216
THE RED RIVER	217
LAO-KAI	220
RACHMED AND A THIBETAN INNKEEPER	221

Across Thibet.

CHAPTER IX.

AMONG THE THIBETANS.

"A Man is Coming"—Description of the First Thibetan Encountered—Thibetan Horsemen—Driving a Bargain—A Savage's First Sight of a Watch—Uncomplimentary Comments—On the High Road to Lhassa—Getting Information under Difficulties—English and Russians in Bad Odour—Lake Burben-cho—The Dungan shows his Seals—Silos—A Thibetan Interior—A Native Woman—Imatch Done Up—Prayers Engraved on Stones—Taking a Prisoner—Death of Imatch—In Sight of the Ningling Tangla and the Namtso.

January 30.—Although we get a little lower down each day, the cold is still intense, the minimum of to-day being 31° below zero at an altitude of 14,200 feet. Still we feel much lighter and walk much more freely, while as we have no longer to concern ourselves in looking for the route, we are able to examine the ridges of the hills more carefully, and see if there is any sign of movement or any spots resembling tents.

January 31.—While the beasts are being loaded and we are sipping our tea in the tent, we hear shouts, and Abdullah comes rushing in, beaming with joy, and says, "You can get out your purse and pay the winner: a man is coming." We enjoin Abdullah to treat the stranger well, give him some tea, take him up to the fire,

THE FIRST THIBETAN ENCOUNTERED.

and try to soften him down and coax what he can out of him. On the arrival of the Thibetan, he is greeted in Mongolian, and replies in the same language, all the men crowding round him and speaking at once. Rachmed comes and tells us that he is ugly beyond description, and that the very bears are better looking. When we think that the ice has been broken, we come out, Prince Henry with his photographic apparatus in his hand, and our presence produces a certain effect upon our guest, as he rises when he sees us, calls us " bembo," that is to say, " chief," and, in order to salute us, lifts up his thumbs and protrudes an enormous tongue, while he bows profoundly. He is begged to sit down again, and we examine him while he is engaged in conversation with Abdullah, if conversation there can be when the two speakers have in common ten words of Mongolian and four of Thibetan.

He is a very little man, with a clean-shaven face covered with a layer of grease and smoke, and furrowed by a great number of deep wrinkles. His eyes, sunken in the orbits, are little more than dark spots beneath the swollen eyelids, the brown pupils are scarcely distinguishable from the discoloured cornea. The face looks narrower than it really is, owing to the long locks of hair which fall down upon the hollow cheeks; the nose is large and the mouth toothless, with thick lips, and the square chin has no sign of hair. The man is weakly, and we can see that his hand is small and dirty, as he manipulates his snuff-box, cut out of a piece of horn, shaking out some powdered red tobacco which he sniffs up into his nose.

His dress is in keeping with his person, his head-gear consisting of a strip of skin which is wound round the forehead and fastened at the back, leaving the top of the head bare. From the crown hangs down a tress of hair, coming as far as the loins and passing through two or three rings made of bones of some beast. The owner of this tress must rub fat over it occasionally, for that portion of his attire against which it rubs is more greasy and shiny than the rest. The sheep-skin pelisse which covers the bare body of our visitor is unspeakably dirty. It would be difficult to say how long he has worn this pelisse, which is fitted to his figure and, in order to facilitate his walking, looped up by means of a cord, so that, about the level of the waist, it forms an enormous fold, which serves as a pocket, from which he extracts his snuff-box, and into which he puts the bread and piece of meat we give him. He also takes out from this pocket a small spinning-wheel, the handle of which is made of polished *orongo* horn and a cross of some wood which we take to be holly. His skinny legs are encased in a pair of woollen stockings, split open at the calf and kept in their place by garters made of hemp, and, like the *espadrillos* of the Spanish mountains, furnished with thick soles.

While asking us as to our journey, the Thibetan takes frequent pinches of snuff or quietly spins the yak wool which he has with him. By means of signs, we explain to him that most of our horses and camels are dead, and that the five or six sheep left have only been allowed to live because there is nothing to eat on them; and we ask him to sell us butter, horses, and sheep. In response to this, he invites us to follow him to his tent, which is beyond the rock that we can see to the westward.

We thank him for his kindness, but beg to be excused, because we want to go to the south-east. Then, with the falsity and impudence of the savage, he endeavours to dissuade us from this by saying that Lhassa is not in that direction, but to the west, asking us, incidentally, and clasping his hands in a reverential manner, if we are going to offer prayers to the Talai Lama. We tell him that we are, and then he again urges us to come and stay a little while in his encampment, where we shall find all kinds of provision and grass for our beasts.

While we are discussing this, we see several flocks descending the slopes of the hills, escorted by men on horseback, who come toward us. The old man gets up as if to go, but we give him another cup of tea, and show him some "iambas" (bars of silver), which we are ready to exchange for sheep. He calls out to a shepherd, who comes trotting up, and explains what we propose, whereupon the latter drives his flock towards us. This second shepherd does not seem to us to be as old as the first, rather taller, and quite as thin. We are struck by the brusqueness of his movements, his irregular gait, his short, quick steps, and a peculiar way of throwing out the knee, giving him the appearance of a being with a human body and the legs of a goat. In fact, one thinks of the monsters of classic mythology as one looks at his long head, his short, snub nose, salient cheek-bones, large mouth from which protrude two teeth that keep the thick lips constantly apart, and enormously developed lower jaw.

He leans upon a long, sharp-pointed lance, which he grasps in a hand black with dirt, and having fingers of nearly equal size; round the waist he carries a sword, the sheath of which is made of wood plated with iron, while the blade is somewhat notched. In order that it may not interfere with his movements on the march, he carries this sword horizontally, and he also has slung over the back a short gun, of small calibre, with a forked rest made of *orongo* horn. The stock is short and square, as is usual with Oriental firearms, and as the gun is fired by means of a fuse, the lance seems the more formidable of the two weapons. Pending the arrival of the flock of sheep, the two Thibetans have a talk, and feel the weight of our bags and chests, and they would carry their indiscretions still farther if we did not, in jest, flourish a revolver at them. This weapon attracts their attention, and they examine its six chambers with manifest surprise, being much astonished at the size of the bullets. When they see that all our men carry a leather case round their waist, they imagine that each of them has his revolver.

The man with the lance asks us if we are from Bomba and Calacata (Bombay and Calcutta), and when we say No, we are people from the West, the Thibetans express their satisfaction, explaining that they are not friends with the people of Bomba and Calacata. They indicate this unfriendliness by joining their index-fingers nail to nail.

In the meanwhile the flock of sheep has come up, in charge of two lads as dirty as their seniors, and in the distance is another person on horseback, whom we find, on looking through the glass, to be a young woman. She is very small, clad in a sheep-skin pelisse coming down to the heels, and bare-headed, her face being hidden in the tresses of her hair. She seems to us to have her cheeks blackened with some kind of unguent.

A lad having failed to lasso one of the sheep which his master picks out from the flock, the latter takes the cord from him and, with surprising quickness, throws it round the horns of a ram. This animal has very fine, silky wool, and a small and well-shaped head, but we reject it, as the flesh would be hard and stringy. The Thibetans are amused at our knowing a good sheep from a bad one, and having, like all savages, first tried to deceive us, show us some fat young sheep, which they secure with the lasso. We pay them in silver bars weighed in Chinese scales, and they examine both the silver and the scales very carefully, and rub the silver with a stone, to see that it contains no lead. Then they break off little bits and put them in their mouths, trying to coax us into giving a few grains more. They are very greedy, and when we exchange a horse which is worn out with fatigue for three sheep, they bargain in a way that shows they are not easily " got over."

We offer to pay them high prices for suitable animals, and they promise to bring us some the next day, showing us at the same time the ponies they are riding. These are such as are bred in the countries of the north, with long coats, and rather short, powerful heads, and when we observe their depth of chest, strong necks, and well-made legs, we do not wonder at their good going. Their masters ride them with a plain halter, never using a bit, their gestures and whip answering every purpose.

These ponies, though they will let their masters do anything with them, are frightened by our strange attire, and will not allow us to come near them and examine their saddles, which are of wood, with very short stirrups not coming below their bellies, so that the rider sits with his knees on the level of his stomach.

After having completed our purchases, we get ready for a start, the Thibetans remaining with us and feeling the canvas of the tent and the texture of our garments, while the English saddles puzzle them not a little as they turn them round and round. They want us to explain to them how we use our weapons, and are astounded at the distance to which a bullet from the Berdane rifle is propelled, though it is clear that the revolvers make the deepest impression upon them.

We put a watch up against the ear of one of the lads, and he is delighted to hear it tick. He looks at the hands, too; but it is the beating of the heart within that chiefly excites his wonder. We take advantage of his friendly attitude to ask him in what direction Lhassa lies, and he points not to the west, like his father, but to the south-east. We reward him with a bit of sugar, which these people appreciate highly, though even to that they would have preferred the canvas of our tent, and some tea and tobacco. Having found that we should not go westward, where, as they say, their tents are, they make off towards the plain with their flocks, whistling and swinging their lassoes.

It is curious to hear the reflections of our men as soon as the Thibetans have gone. A few days ago you might have sworn that they would have taken any of their fellow-men into their affections, but now they make the most uncomplimentary comments on the ugliness and dirtiness of these natives, their greed and their suspiciousness. The young woman with her besmeared face is described as a monster, and only the sheep and horses are exempt from unfavourable criticism. Nevertheless, the spirits of our men have improved, and the downheartedness and despair engendered by solitude have disappeared, as I can see this evening when our tent is pitched in the middle of a river-bed partly dry. They are anxious to guard against being taken by surprise and attacked at night, and the tents are placed in a triangular shape, so that a look-out may be kept in all directions, while the horses and camels are hobbled and placed in the centre of the camp. Arms are examined and well greased, and we shall sleep with our guns out of their cases. For have we not come again upon our brethren, part of the great human family?

We are on the high road to Lhassa; of that there can be no doubt, and the certainty will save us a great deal of trouble, for the farther we go the better marked the route will be. The worst part of the business is that our animals are nearly done up, and that several of our men have great difficulty in advancing. Old Imatch is the worst, his feet being frost-bitten. One of his big toes is nearly dropping off, and his sores are so dreadful that it is a wonder he can keep on his horse. He is constantly suffering from mountain sickness, and we can do nothing to relieve it, for what he needs is his native steppe on the level of the sea, which he will probably never see again.

If we could only come upon a suitable spot to halt and nurse him! But the whole of this region is the same; it is a lofty steppe, inhabited by a few wretched nomads, with the west wind constantly blowing. Our stages are short, for although the route is as good as could be desired, we cannot go more than twelve miles a day without fatiguing poor Imatch, while Abdullah is a bad walker, and Parpa is so weak that he can scarcely follow the camels.

If we had a few vigorous and determined men, we might, by a *coup de main*, seize as many of the Thibetans' horses as we require, load them, and march direct on Lhassa. But there are not enough of us, and we must resign ourselves to dragging along and awaiting more favourable circumstances.

February 1.—This morning, with a west wind and a cloudy sky, we came in sight of a flock of yaks and sheep making for the region we had just traversed. Not one of them came our way, and perhaps some kind friend has told the herdsmen we want animals of different kinds and are armed to the teeth!

Just as we were loading and about to start, not reckoning that our friends of yesterday would bring us the animals we offered to buy, five horsemen appeared in sight, pulled up at a distance of two or three hundred yards, put the horses in charge of one of their number, and came on foot into our camp. We recognise the little old man of yesterday, and he again very politely puts out his tongue, and is imitated by his companions, whom we had not seen before. One of them has an aquiline profile, his pigtail is ornamented with agates, inferior turquoises, and copper rings, and his pelisse is edged with leopard-skin. These people place at our feet a small jar of milk, which emits an odour sufficient to prevent any of us making a rush for it, a piece of rancid butter rolled up in a piece of skin, and a small bag of *zamba* or roasted barley-meal.

They examine us with great curiosity, but are very reserved in their replies to our questions, and display remarkable rapacity. The old man, whom we ask about the horses he has promised us, says that there are none, for they have gone off westward. We can get nothing out of these fellows, who pretend not to understand whenever we pronounce the names of Lhassa, Namtso, or Ningling Tangla. Fortunately, one of them is less suspicious, or more intelligent, and while the others are having their attention drawn off, we enter into negotiations with this poor wretch, who is very scantily clad, and has the profile of a negro, with scarcely perceptible eyes, and the forehead of a child. We begin by offering him a lump of sugar, one or two dried apricots, and some raisins, all of which he thinks delicious. Then we tell him that we are going to offer prayer to the Talai-Lama, where-

TALKING OVER THE FIRST THIBETANS (p. 4).

upon the fervent Thibetan at once throws his cap to the ground, falls on to his knees, clasps his hands, and turns instinctively in the direction of Lhassa, as he mumbles his "Om mane padmé houm," which we repeat after him. We explain that all the contents of our chests are for the Talai-Lama, and he at once approves of this, nothing being too good for that divinity; but at the same time he stretches out his hand and makes a gesture as of eating. So we give him some more apricots, and crack the stone of one, showing him how to get at the kernel. He imitates the operation, and makes a movement of satisfaction with his tongue.

Then, pointing to the direction in which he was prostrating himself just now, we whisper—

"Lhassa?"

And he, first looking to see whether his companions are watching him, makes an affirmative motion with his head. We then said to him, in Thibetan, "How many days to Lhassa?" But instead of answering, he put out his hand for a piece of sugar, then, having hidden himself behind our tent, he traced on the sand a curved line in a south-easterly direction and placed some *argol*, at the end of the line, saying, as he put his finger on it, "Lhassa."

Then we speak to him about the great salt deposit of Burben-cho, as it is called on the maps, and which he pronounced "Boultso;" whereupon he placed another piece of dung on the curved line. When we pronounced the name of Namtso (the Tengri Nor of the Mongols), he put an *argol* upon the curved line a little farther; and when we suddenly say, "Ningling Tangla," he falls on his knees, places an *argol* to the south of Lake Namtso, and prays fervently to the holy mountain. He gets up and puts out his hand for another and yet another apricot, and, by way of thanking us, opens a mouth like that of a crocodile, from which he protrudes a massive tongue like that of an ox, covering the whole of his chin. Father Dedeken thinks it would fill the whole of an ox-tongue tin.

He is gradually getting more familiar, and in reply to our inquiries says it is three days' journey to Boultso, eight to Namtso, and twelve to Lhassa.

If he is speaking the truth, as seems probable, his estimates refer to the time he himself took on the journey, not to the time we should take. We find it difficult to get rid of him, so greedy is he for more apricots; but he goes at last, and, despite the amiable invitation of the Thibetans to visit their camp to the west, we follow the route leading south-east. It traverses the steppe coated with snow; and as the horizon is misty, we see no high chain, only ridges divided by valleys, in which domesticated flocks are roaming not far from wild animals. Now and again we catch a glimpse of black tents, and over them "prayers" fluttering from the end of a pole; but we do not approach any of these dwellings, as they are some way off the road.

February 2.—A body of horsemen, well mounted, and all of them armed, after watching us from a distance, draw near. Greetings are exchanged, and we try to persuade them to sell us some horses. They look at the silver, but do not reply, so, being anxious to know what they mean, we take possession of an animal which would suit us. Its owner remains with us, but the others go off; and when we name a price, the Thibetan refuses, explaining that the "Bembo," or chief, would punish him if he sold the horse without permission. So we let him go, after having made him a present and urged him to bring us plenty of *zamba* for our animals. He replies that he will be willing enough, but that only the "Bembo" can decide.

February 3.—Two natives come to offer us some dried sheep carcases, and after a good deal of preliminary fencing we obtain information. According to one of these men, the route goes through the plain as far as Ningling Tangla, and there is plenty of grass, ice, and snow. He seems to be unusually intelligent, as he endeavours to let Father Dedeken understand him by pronouncing with great distinctness the names of the places he mentions. He was rendered thus loquacious by the present of a handglass, and the promise of a small chromo-lithograph if he spoke the truth stimulated his desire to be of use. As he rode along by our side, we passed some camel-droppings, and on our asking him what these were, he replied, "Tangout," this being the name given to the Kalmucks; so that we have come again upon the traces of our pilgrims at the same time that we have discovered the high road. He gave us to understand that there is no more direct route than this to Lhassa. One soon gets used to these barbarian physiognomies, for we begin to detect intelligence in this vendor of dried meat. As he accompanied us to our bivouac, and night set in, we invited him to stay with our men, but he preferred going off to his *kiim* (dwelling) after letting his horse browse on a few roots of grass. The moon was up, and he pointed to it, as much as to say he should be able to find his way. He thanked us effusively, with uplifted thumbs and protruding tongue, for all the presents we had given him; and when we gave him back the meat we did not want, and told him to keep the price of it, he prostrated himself and explained that our generosity was well placed, because "those you saw yesterday are the chiefs, and I am poor." So there are rich and poor everywhere.

With bright moonlight and a light westerly breeze, we have a minimum of 24° below zero, and no longer camp in sheltered corners, but on elevated places, where we at once command the plain and are sufficiently removed from the heights to have time to fire several shots at horsemen who might gallop down on us.

We have some excellent watch-dogs, that keep us informed of all that is going on in the camp. One of them, a mastiff with a long red coat, is in the habit of sleeping at a distance of over

300 feet from the camp, and of keeping on the watch all night, so that it would be he who would warn the two *bassels* set to look after the tents. These excellent animals seem to understand the importance of their task, and will not let any Thibetan come near without our permission, so we can sleep in perfect peace.

February 4.—This morning their barking announced the approach of some twenty horsemen, who halted at a distance of about a third of a mile, pitched their tent, unsaddled their horses, and settled themselves. Two of them came towards us, but the dogs kept them at a distance, and they sat down and made signs, as if to ask for an audience. The dogs having been called in, one of the visitors opened the conversation in Mongolian with Abdullah, who had been taught what to say; and when the Thibetans asked where we came from, he replied, "From the North."

"Where are you going?"

"In search of a good place."

"What are you doing?"

"We have come on the chase, and we have been led on towards the south. Our horses and camels are dying of hunger, and even some of our men have died. We are very tired, and should like to rest."

"Stay here."

"Here, and eat the stones! Until we have found a good place we shall not stop."

"What is your country?"

"We are men of the West."

"You are Pa-Lan, no doubt?"

"No."

"Ah, if you are Pa-Lan, I shall get into trouble if I let you pass. Come and talk with us in our tent."

"I must ask permission of my chiefs."

Abdullah came and told us what had occurred, and received permission to go and converse with the ambassadors, though he was strictly cautioned to keep a watch over his words and to appear ignorant when asked any awkward question. On his return he reported that the men said that on the first day of our arrival they sent a letter to Lhassa asking for orders, and that the reply had come—

"If they are Pa-Lan" (that is, English or Russians), "let them not come farther, but let them be supplied with what they require for returning. If they are not Pa-Lan, ask them for their passport and send them on to Lhassa."

The Thibetan chief expressed a wish to have an interview with the chief of our party, but Abdullah put him off by saying that his chief was taking his rest; adding, "When he is ready, I will inform you, and then you can come and bring him some butter." When the Thibetans did come, Abdullah said, "You are too petty chiefs to converse with ours; but if you will sell some horses, we will buy them of you; if not, you may be off." Whereupon they went off without saying anything, and sat down about a hundred yards away.

In the meanwhile we packed our things and went on our way, arriving by a pass of 15,700 feet upon a plateau, at the foot of which, to the east, is a rather large lake, which we supposed to be the "Burben-cho," as the shores were covered with salt, and we had been told the water of this lake was so salt that one could not keep it in the mouth.

We closed in as we drew near this lake, for numerous detachments of armed horsemen appeared on the ridges, some of whom advanced towards us. When the stragglers came up, we encamped to the west of the lake, near a frozen spring, the water of which is drinkable, and which receives the downpour from the hills, where most of the Thibetan horsemen are going to pass the night. They will be about a third of a mile from us, and we can see them lighting their fires and wandering about the plain to pick up *argol*.

The Boultso, or Burben-cho, runs back into the mountains, where it seems to form gulfs. So, at least, we judge, for the sunshine transforms it into some resemblance to the Lake of Lucerne.

TENT AT BURBEN-CHO (p. 29).

But this view is incorrect, for it is evident that we are the victims of the mirage, and that the water we fancy we can see in the distance does not exist.

The Burben-cho is a vast salt-pit enveloping what remains of a lake, judging by what is seen on the banks. At the foot of the platform, which was perhaps the shore to which the water formerly attained, we find the traces of numerous camels, and by the footmarks it is clear they must have remained several days. It is probable that the Torgots sojourned here and pastured their animals, for the grass is cropped very close, and ours do not find anything to eat. There is, moreover, a total lack of snow.

When we unload, the Thibetans come close up, and we

THIBETANS AT BURBEN-CHO.

recognise among them the meat-vendors of the previous day, but we pretend not to see them, and leave the dogs to keep them at a distance. So they return to their rocks, where they will pass the night. They walk along very slowly, in conversation, and I have no trouble in catching them up. I am anxious to get a close view of them and to make the acquaintance of the old man whom our interpreter describes as their chief. He is a little, old man, dressed like his subjects and quite as dirty, but he has a nose which seems as if it were formed of three enormous mulberries, one representing the tip and the two others the nostrils. This magisterial appendix, flanked by two small but intelligent eyes, does not detract from the good-natured expression of his face, round which his long hair flows in a fashion that reminds one of the wig worn by the Grand Monarque. We look at each other with keen interest, and having greeted Mongolian fashion, "Sen Béné, Sen Béné!." I give him my card, in the shape of a lump of sugar. He eyes me, mumbling something I cannot catch, and his companions, whenever I look at them, turn their eyes away with alarm. One of them attracts my special attention, for he is thin and lanky, with hair hanging down his cheeks, an elongated neck, and emaciated face—quite the type of the *scholasticus* in the farces of the Middle Ages. I can scarcely help laughing when I look at him; but he is stiff and upright, and turns his face away from mine, half in terror, half in disgust, muttering "Pa-Lan, Pa-Lan," as if I were some sort of unclean animal. They look at me again for a moment, and then make off with the short rapid steps which are peculiar to them, while their looped-up pelisses flap against their thighs like petticoats.

February 5.—The cold is still intense, the minimum of last night being 22° below zero; but the wind has gone down. This morning the old chief with a Louis XIV. head of hair returns, escorted by twenty Thibetans. He again explains to the interpreter what a delicate position he is in, and that he will be punished if he lets us through. Why could we not await the orders from Lhassa in a nice place where we should get grass, fresh meat, water, and everything we could desire? He would like to present his respects to us in person; but we decline to receive him until he has sold us some horses. We want them, and if he is well-disposed, that is the best way of showing it. To this he replies that he will sell or even give us sheep, but that he dares not let us have horses without an order.

Father Dedeken then goes to see him, and the old man offers him three lumps of fat sewn up in a skin, which he places upon a light scarf (called "the scarf of happiness") spread upon the ground, putting the other end of the scarf upon Father Dedeken's knee. The latter asks him if this salt-pit is really the Burben-cho, and the old man taps him on the arm, as much as to say, "Don't make fun of me; you know the country as well as I do."

He is very puzzled to know what to make of us, for we have no Thibetans in our troop, and have arrived by a route which he does not know himself, while we have no guide, and our band is composed of men of various races in strange dress. We go along without asking our way, halting near the ice at places where others have already encamped, as if we were going over ground we had traversed before. He then goes to the Dungan, and shows him documents, with Chinese seals affixed to them, which confer upon him the police powers he exercises. Then, thinking to touch our camel-driver in a weak point, he adds—

"You say that you are Chinese, but every respectable Chinaman travels with his papers in order, and cannot leave the country without the permission of his mandarins. There is no saying what your antecedents are."

This is too much for the Dungan, who pounces upon the bag in which his papers are put away, unfolds them, and puts them under the nose of the old Thibetan.

"There! Have you any such papers as these? Now do you believe that I am an honest man? Compare your papers with mine. Your papers are those of a nobody—mine are very different. My seals are double the size of yours, and my passports were delivered by great mandarins, but your diploma does not signify anything. By what right do you meddle with my affairs, or dare to speak in such a way to a man who has in his possession passports with seals of this size?"

The argument of the seals is too much for the Thibetan, who goes off dumfounded. It is evident that these people do not know who we are, and that they will not come to any decision until they do. It is to our advantage not to enlighten them, as we can do without their assistance.

So we march on through the bare steppe and climb a range of hills, near the summit of which we encamp, beside a pass and not far from an abundant spring which descends, in the form of ice, towards the eastern part of the valley. On the other side of the ice we see a black tent; and as it is the first we have come within reach of, go to have a look at it, and are greeted by the barking of four black dogs, which show their teeth, and seem disposed to attack us but are called off by two people who come out of the tent. One of these is very old, and is led by the other, who is very diminutive. The elder, bent by years, has a head which, with its close-cropped grey hair, reminds me of the "Diogenes" of Velasquez. He has small weak eyes, out of which he can scarcely see, and he takes Father Dedeken for a Chinaman, and greets him with the word "Loïé." His companion is a girl of about eight, who would perhaps be pretty if she were cleaner; but it is evident that she has never been washed, her round face, with its imperceptible nose, being a mixture of black and yellow. Her dress is a sheepskin, with a piece of wool to tie it in at the waist; and she carries a small knife in a leather sheath at her side. Bareheaded like the old man, she wears her hair loose down her back, with a plait twisted over the forehead.

We re-conduct the aged lama—for such we recognise him to be by his close-cropped hair—back to his dwelling, and, after we have given him some dried fruits, we begin to converse. He assures us that the salt-pit near which we encamped yesterday was the Burben-cho, and tells us that the chain of mountains is called

TIBETAN HORSEMEN.

the Burben-cho Ré (the mountain of Burben-cho), and that the Namtso is at four days' march by a very easy route. This poor old man is very amiable, and we ask him for some milk, as we see that he has numerous yaks feeding lower down, but he says the grass is so bare that they are now nearly dry.

Their tent is made of a sort of black woollen stuff, and it covers a surface of about four yards square; it is kept up at the corners by pegs that are attached to other pegs by means of long ropes that can either be pulled taut or loosened as required. The black mass from which all these ropes are stretched has the aspect of a vast spider with an eye in the back, this being the opening for the smoke at the top. The door of the tent is to the east, owing to the prevalence of westerly winds, protection against which is afforded by a high wall of *argol*, which is much used for constructions of various kinds.

While looking over this domain we observe what appear to be round ovens, or mounds coming about up to one's waist. These are silos, constructed of *argol* on the level of the soil, probably because it would be difficult to dig into it, and they contain bits of stuff, tufts of wool, and even high, broad-brimmed hats, or head-dresses, while yak-skins are spread out near the tent, close to small round pots of red earth. Slabs of schist, with prayers engraved on them, are deposited behind the tent; that is to say, in the direction of the west wind, which is supposed to utter them as it goes by.

Some distance off is the site of an abandoned tent, which enables us to form an idea of what a Thibetan interior is like. A number of stones are put together in a square, and form a sort of substructure for the tent. In the centre is an oven made of clay and flat stones, while in the corner is a box for holding *argol*, where we in France should have one for fire-wood. The saddle and mill are of the most primitive kind, and among other objects are a basket made of withies and the skull of a yak converted into a vase. A few round stones have been used as pestles or hammers, while the objects the owners have wished to keep and use again on their return have been put away in one of the silos. Another contains a great many droppings of lambs, and it is doubtless in these places that the lambs are sheltered, while their parents sleep in the open.

February 6.—The light being bad yesterday, it was not till this morning that Prince Henry could photograph this dwelling, and the operation was a more complicated one than might be imagined, for it was necessary to keep clear of the dogs and, if possible, get a portrait of the inhabitants.* We have great difficulty in beating off the angry dogs, when a man with a long nose and a very high forehead comes out and calls them off by throwing them bits of dried yak; and while we are getting the apparatus ready, a woman's head peers out from behind the curtain of the tent. She is quite a caricature of a human being, her profile being that of a monkey, just touched up so as to make her slightly resemble a woman. By dint of giving her plenty of raisins, peaches, and apricots, we get her to put out the rest of her body, and, urged on by the old man whose acquaintance we made yesterday, she stands at the door, holding her daughter by the hand. She is very diminutive in stature, and clad of course in sheepskin. Her eyes are horizontal, and the pupil is a mere speck of brown merged in a very dark-stained cornea almost as brown; the cheek-bones are prominent, the chin broad and protruding. She keeps her mouth open, her thick lips being puckered up, so that she has a good-humoured but unintelligent smile. Her hair, parted on the forehead, falls down over her cheeks and back in small tresses ornamented with stones and shells, and tied together at the ends with a bit of ribbon. She cannot be called good-looking, but we have succeeded in

---

* M. Bonvalot does not say the occupants of the tent had returned during the night, but this is to be inferred.—*Translator's Note.*

winning her goodwill and that of the men of her family, for when we give her another bit of sugar, she and the man stretch out their thumbs and clasp their hands, this being their way of saying a friendly good-bye.

After going eastwards along the chain of Bur-ben-cho, we made a bend to the south-east, where we came upon the route which we had momentarily lost sight of, and encamped in a valley near some tents, where we met with a rather unfriendly reception from both men and dogs. We succeeded, however, in getting a little *argol*; but as to milk, it was impossible to obtain a drop, the yaks not yielding any.

It is high time, nevertheless, that the Thibetans should show us a little good-

A PETTY CHIEF (p. 27).

will, for old Imatch is quite done up. He cannot stand, and can only creep along on his knees. He has to be helped on to his horse, and yesterday he begged us to abandon him on the route, saying that he was doomed, and could be of no further use to us. We do the best we can, but are powerless to relieve him. Parpa has fallen down several times during the day's march, and we have had to go and fetch him with a camel at a hundred yards from the bivouac, which he could not reach.

Little Abdullah is not much better; he can only get along by holding on to the girth of a camel, and is incapable of carrying his gun. We absolutely must have horses, and shall seize them at the first opportunity.

February 8.—Last night a south-westerly wind blew with great violence, and this morning our men complain of headache and singing in the ears, while Imatch and the others who are ill groan lamentably. So we start in poor spirits for the pass, the summit of which is indicated by an *obo*.

Orders have no doubt been sent to the Thibetans, for the flocks have been dispersed since daybreak, and we cannot get within reach of the horses; while in the tents we pass, there are only old people, women, and children, the men, with their arms, having made off. It is evident that a void is being made around us, and though so far we have been very gentle in our dealings, we must now resort to other methods.

At the foot of the pass, near a frozen stream, we saw three men eating *zamba*, which they were cooking at an *argol*-fire. We went up to them and asked for a horse for a sick man. They feigned not to understand, and would not even look at the money we offered them; but as their horses were close by, we took one for Parpa, and kept them at a distance with our revolvers.

February 9.—During the night the sheep purchased from the first lot of Thibetans were stolen. We are determined that whenever we require fresh meat we will take it.

The pass is 17,300 feet high, and the descent an easy one, leading to a valley in which we see, for the first time, white tents, occupied by armed men. As soon as they notice us they run off to collect their horses, which are roaming about. At the foot of the pass we see—also for the first time—a large number of prayers engraved upon the stones, as mentioned by Father Huc, in his description of the high road of the pilgrims. It is clear, therefore, that we are drawing near to the holy city.

I should have mentioned that on the 8th about forty armed horsemen hovered about our camp, and the old man with the bulbous nose who speaks Mongolian came with another chief better dressed than himself, and almost clean. He begged us to halt, "for our lives were at stake." We asked him to cease joking at a time when two of our men were very ill.

Climbing another pass, we can see from the top, despite the mist and the dust, a corner of the great lake below us; and to the south, much farther up, some white peaks, which seem to emerge from a formidable chain, not impossibly the Ningling Tangla. We are approaching a group of mountains, the passes are more numerous, and the route follows valleys a mile or two wide, the country having the aspect of the Pamir.

The west wind tries us very much, but, nevertheless, it seems as if winter were about to end, for we have seen a flight of pigeons and another of sparrows. Wild asses and antelopes abound, and we notice a number of small lakes which are gradually drying up, their shores being white with salt.

February 10.—We are now in a steppe covered in many places with stones, and here and there with grass. While scaling yet another pass, we again come upon very distinct footmarks of camels dating from last year.

February 11.—We traverse a valley which is a marsh during the rainy season, and in the course of the march receive a visit from a Thibetan chief who seems to us to be tipsy. He wears a red cloak and boots of the same colour, and carries in his hand a prayer-mill with plates of silver on it, which he turns incessantly. He has come all the way to say to us in Mongolian, "Tengri mo sen, ta mo sen, char mo sen;" which means, "Sky not good, horse not good, town not good." Thereupon he galloped off, having told us nothing new, except that some Mongolian pilgrims must have made a stay in his country, for he had picked up a few words of their language.

February 12.—A violent west wind seals the fate of poor old Imatch. He sobs when the time comes for starting, and sending for Parpa says: "You remember that I am in your debt. At Tcharkalik I bought some boots of you, and did not pay for them. If Allah pleases to let me get better, I will pay you for them. If I die, you will pay yourself with what I have left, and keep the rest; for you gave me to drink during the night."

I try to cheer him up by saying that we shall soon reach a town, and that we are all fond of him, and anxious to nurse him. He says: "Thank you, and forgive me if I do not attend to my work. But I cannot. Death is at hand, and has already taken possession of my legs. Forgive me. I will not sob any more. I will not give way to despair. It is all over."

We get the poor fellow mounted as best we can, and start very downhearted, resuming our course to the south-east. For the first time we see upon the heads of three very ugly women a tall head-dress, not unlike a pope's tiara. Our stage, though longer than that of yesterday, in order that we may encamp near a lake, is only ten miles, so exhausted are we.

A number of sheep are feeding close by, and as, whenever we try to speak to the natives, they make off, we determine to kill some of the flock for our personal use. The old woman who is in charge of them makes off, uttering piercing shrieks. Rachmed has had the good sense to pick out some fine fat lambs. In the rough ground near the lake we see some men encamped, with five or six horses close at hand, and Prince Henry and myself determine to try and seize them. The Thibetans make a dash to be off, but not in time to prevent our securing one of their horses, their leader, and one of his men. Their weapons had been laid down in a heap, and they did not make any effort to prevent us seizing them, but were up on their horses and off. We fired a few shots from a revolver after them, which only quickened their flight.

The old man whom we have made prisoner sits dazed, and puts out his tongue in a most beseeching way. He has a lot of small bags containing provisions, and he offers us in turn, by way of mollifying us, handfuls of powdered cheese, *zamba*, and dried meat. These we refuse, and he sits there muttering prayers and

LAKE NAMTSO (p. 32).

looking at us with evident anxiety and fear. After letting him be alarmed for the moment, we proceed, when the rest of our men have come up, to explain that if we want horses it is because several of our men cannot walk, and that we are prepared to pay a good price, while he raises his thumb by way of satisfaction when we call him "appa," "popeunn" ("father," "brother").

Our dogs alarm him very much, and he begs us to call them away; but we reassure him by saying that they do not bite those whom we call "brothers." Then we give him a supply of sugar, and when he has tasted it he cannot hide his satisfaction, while after he has had some raisins and apricots, he in turn calls us "brothers." Then we show him silver bars, and bargain with him for his horse, while, to prove that our intentions are good, we set his companion at liberty and allow him to carry off his pelisse. The latter jumps at the offer, and skelters off without any concern for his master.

At this juncture a horseman arrives with a red pendant fastened to the barrel of his gun. He says that he is the owner of the sheep killed by Rachmed, and we at once offer him some tea, which he drinks out of a cup done up in his pelisse, as his religion forbids men of his race to let their lips touch anything which impure lips have approached. This may appear singular to Europeans, and is perhaps only a preventive against certain contagious diseases, very necessary in a country where the crockery is never washed.

In the meanwhile a silver bar has been taken out of a bag and shown to him. He asks to be allowed to test it; and when we tell him that the stamp which he has noticed is Pekin, he seems reassured, and repeats "Pétsin, Pétsin." Nevertheless, when we weigh him out the price of his lambs, he again examines the money before putting it into a small bag hanging round his neck. When we give him a small handglass, he does not at first understand its use; but when the chief, our prisoner, sees himself in it, he laughs almost like an idiot, and explains the secret to his friend, the latter going off in high glee. The prisoner himself is quite at ease, and asks to be allowed to sleep where he is, only begging us to keep off the dogs and let him have a mirror. This we promise, and in the meanwhile pay him for his horse, which we fasten up close to our tents.

February 13.—Our dogs barked all night, and were answered by others in the distance, while in the semi-darkness that precedes day the wolves were howling dolefully. At this moment, as I go out of the tent, Rachmed comes to say that Imatch has just died. Yesterday, when I asked him how he was, he replied "Better," and, though his breath was short and his face swollen, he drank his tea with pleasure. He took an interest, too, in what was going on in the tent, and I had noticed him putting *argols* on the fire, from sheer force of habit, like the true man of the steppe he was. Placing him near the entrance to the tent, which was his favourite place, we had rolled him well up in his pelisse and rugs, and he had stretched himself out to sleep. When asked if there was anything he would like, he said "No," and we did not think his end was so near. Rachmed's account of his last moments was as follows:—

"When the wolves howled, Imatch called out, 'Parpa, give me some water; I am thirsty.' To which Parpa replied, 'The water is frozen, but I will go and light a fire and melt some ice for you to drink.' Then, when the ice was ready, Imatch drank it without help, but with some difficulty, and said how glad he was to quench his last thirst. Then he stretched himself out and began to groan a little. All at once he jumped up, went out of the tent on his knees, and returned to his couch. We got the tea ready, and offered him a cup as soon as it was made. But he could not keep down the first mouthful, and, putting back the cup, he called us all—'Timour, Iça, Abdullah, Parpa, Rachmed!' We all gathered round him, and, raising himself on his elbow, he uttered the following words, broken by sighs: 'I shall not arrive. Allah will not take me any farther. Good-bye. I am very pleased with you all. You have taken great care of me. Good-bye. I am gone!' He fell back, and in a moment his spirit had fled."

Such is the narrative to which we listen by the glimmer of our lantern, for day has not yet dawned, and as soon as it is light we will bury him in a hollow spot down in the quagmire. Imatch had followed us all the way from Djarkent, from the frontier of Siberia. We all liked him; for if he was rough of speech, he was good-hearted, plucky, and a hard worker. He took great care of his camels, which had formerly belonged to him in part; but having fallen into the clutches of a usurer, he had to sell them and become the servant of his creditor, who had sold them to us for at least double what he had paid Imatch for them. As we paid him high wages, he reckoned upon being able to purchase back his camels and "become Imatch himself again," as he put it.

But Allah had decided otherwise, and the poor Kirghis will not see his native steppe again. We lay him in the earth, wrapped in the felt which served him for a bed. We turn his face to the south-east, and our men bring stones and earth to cover his body, while prayers are recited with the accompaniment of sobs and tears.

Then we prepare to start for the Namtso, which, according to our prisoner, whom we set at liberty, giving him presents, and letting him have the arms we captured yesterday, is on the other side of a chain of hills over which our road leads. The certainty that the Tengri Nor—the Namtso, as the Thibetans say—is there, gives us fresh vigour, and we only regret our horses cannot follow us. Father Dedeken and Prince Henry have to abandon theirs, and only two were destined to reach the holy lake.

When we get to the summit of the pass, we perceive the Ningling Tangla and the eastern extremity of the lake, and we scale the neighbouring heights, so as to take in a wider horizon. At our feet, between cliffs to the west, from which descend promontories, forming gulfs and bays, the lake glitters like a beautiful silver mirror, round in shape, but oval like an egg. To the south-west the lake skirts a hill, and extends much farther; but whether this hill forms part of an island or a peninsula we cannot tell. The Ningling Tangla arrests our attention much longer, as this chain unfolds before us its summits and peaks capped with snow, quite shutting out the horizon. We are struck by the nearly equal altitude of this long row of peaks, surmounting spurs which descend towards the lake in regular rows like the tents of an encamped army; and just in the centre we can see, towering over all the rest, four large icy peaks which the Thibetans revere, for behind them is Lhassa, the "city of the spirits."

Descending the stony and sandy slope, we reached the shores of the lake. Looking at the lake from the northern side, we did not see any snow upon the ridge which skirts it, whereas the Ningling Tangla is quite white, thus illustrating the Thibetan saying, "The water of the Namtso is made of the snow of the Ningling Tangla."

As we go southward the lake seems to open out in a south-westerly direction; and as long as the mist prevents us from seeing the end of it, we might take it to be a boundless sea. The evening sun, striking the ice, makes it sparkle like jewels; and we can well appreciate the origin of its name, "the lake of heaven."

PACK HORSES.

CHAPTER X.

AWAITING ORDERS FROM LHASSA.

At Namtso—Encamping Near Ningling Tangla Pass—An Embassage—The Thibetans Undecided—The Caravan in Battle Array—A Mandarin—A Mongolian Interpreter—Arrival of the Amban from Lhassa—Giving Him Audience—His Suite and Their Costumes—A Long Interview—The Thibetans' New Year's Day—In the Amban's Tent—Gibeonites—Another Mongolian Interpreter—The Apathy of Thibetans—A Storm—Arrival of the Ta-Lama and the Ta-Amban—Plain Speaking—Refusal to Return—The Ta-Lama and the Ta-Amban Described—Abdullah and the Dungan at their Devotions—Colloquy between Rachmed and Timour—Thibetans at Work—Their General Characteristics—Carnivorous Horses—The Samda Kansain Mountains—The Samda Tchou River—A Blade of Grass—How They do Business at Lhassa.

RELIGIOUS INSIGNIA.

Our arrival at Namtso is an important event for us. Although we are the first Europeans actually to behold it, it is marked on the maps, thanks to the researches of the pundit Nain-Singh. At last we are safe out of the unknown country in which we have been since leaving the pass of Amban Ashkan Dawan, and we know now where we are. This thought would cheer us but for the pitiful condition of our little troop, for our camels have no strength, and all means of transport will soon fail us.

We purpose staying here a day, not so much to rest our beasts—for they are too far gone to enjoy a rest—as to prolong their lives a little by letting them feed on the grass which surrounds our camp pretty thickly. Up till now we have not seen the envoys of the authorities at Lhassa, a fact which causes us no little astonishment, for they ought to have been advised of our arrival some time ago, our stages having been very short ones since we first met with the men, and couriers having had plenty of time to convey the information.

It is probable, however, that we shall very soon have an opportunity of demanding an explanation from the natives, for a movement is visible in the little plain formed by the old bed of the lake. Bodies of men on horseback are passing at some distance from our camp, and are going south. Their intention, doubtless, is to gather at the pass by which we shall try to climb the Ningling Tangla. I say advisedly "shall try," for a worn-out band can attempt nothing with any assurance of success. Should we encounter a difficult road, we should have to stop, unless favoured by luck, which it does not do to count upon. We are not reduced, however, to the last extremity, for we have still provisions, meat, and tea enough for several months, besides sugar, preserved vegetables, and ammunition, while deer, ptarmigan, and wild asses are within shooting range, and make excellent food. But strength is failing, both in man and beast.

We pass the day shooting, and besides the meat of the wild asses, which we procure in this way, we enrich our collection of lammergeiers and vultures. On the borders of the lake we notice the steam from hot salt-springs, amidst the rocks which rise at the north end. Here and there some stunted junipers are growing. It is a long time since we have seen any semblance of vegetation, and our men literally shout for joy. Our instruments tell us that we are at an altitude of 15,321 feet, this being very near to the estimate of Naïn-Singh, who puts it at 15,400 feet.

February 15.—To-day we do another ten miles to the south, crossing at the head of the lake a river which runs into it. This river divides into several small arms which thaw during a part of the day only, and that merely on the surface, so that the water flows on the top of the ice. Whilst crossing it some of us have an unexpected foot-bath, a thing to which we have for a long time been strangers.

We proceeded to set up our tents not far from the pass which crosses the Ningling Tangla, on the east of which are some magnificent peaks, the highest two of which we christened Huc and Gabet, in memory of the courageous missionaries who penetrated to Lhassa.

On the other side of the ice we were awaited by some of the horsemen whom we had seen, and amongst their number was one who spoke a little Mongolian. He was in the midst of a group of men whose costume, which was comparatively clean, showed them to be chiefs. All round us were scattered, at a respectful distance, numerous small bands, making several hundred men in all, so that we closed up our ranks and grasped our rifles. The first use we made of the interpreter, who approached to present his superiors to us, was to ask him to inform his compatriots that we should fire on any horsemen who approached us, and that consequently they would do well to keep their distance until we had seen the "great chiefs" with whom we wished to speak, and from whom we should learn whether we were in a friendly or hostile country. We added that, according to the custom of our own country, it would be becoming to wait until we had pitched our tents before conversing, and at the same time, with our whips, we scattered several who had come too close.

When we had pitched our tents on a slight elevation to the left of the road, the ambassadors came up and were received by Dedeken and Abdullah at the fire of the Dungan. Their first business was to hand us, as presents, some packets of rancid butter and a stone bottle, of European manufacture, containing a spirit made from barley, and not unpalatable. They then informed us, through Akoun, that they had been sent from Lhassa to ask us who we were. During the conversation we examined their horses, which seemed excellent. Their baggage was transported by mules, which were very strong, though of small build. After some time, through one of our men, they asked permission to visit us, but we refused on the plea that we did not speak their language, and that they were not of sufficiently high rank. It is absolutely necessary to give people a high opinion of yourself when you are travelling in the East and meet with strangers. As they quitted the camp we saw that they were well-clothed, in the Chinese fashion, that they were taller and stouter than those of their fellow-countrymen whom we had so far come across, and that, from their polished manners, they evidently belonged to a town.

Dedeken and Abdullah reported their conversation to us. They presented themselves to us as envoys of the Talai Lama and of the Amban of Lhassa, the former being the highest religious authority, and the latter one of the greatest civic personages, a sort of Under-Secretary of State. They wished to see our papers, to know who we were, for what purpose we were travelling, etc. By way of answer to these questions we complained of the manner in which we had been received *en route;* adding that we could not obtain any help, purchase provisions, or hire beasts of burden; that we failed to understand such treatment, seeing that we had paid generously for what we had bought on the first day, but that, notwithstanding, we had been obliged to seize things by force; and that if they continued to treat us as highwaymen, we should behave as such. Thereupon a lama, clad in yellow silk and decorated with the bright blue button, spoke volubly and expressed his regrets that we had been so treated, begging us to understand that no one looked for proper behaviour from savages, from "Si fantse," assuring us at the same time that we should, for the future, have no cause to complain. Finally, he urged us to hand him our papers, and to remain where we were, when our wants would be supplied. Dedeken replied that we had need of rest, and that we wished to stop at a more convenient spot. Abdullah made us laugh by repeating the illustrations he had used when speaking to these savages, as, when he handed them sugar and bade them remark its whiteness, "Such is the whiteness of our intentions," or, when they drank their tea, "You like it, though, before you drank it, you did not like it. So will it be with us: when you have made our acquaintance you will like us as much as you do the tea."

We comment on the events of the day, seated round our pot, in which the rancid butter they have given us is melting and emitting a somewhat disagreeable odour. We come to the conclusion that the Thibetans do not know what to decide, and that their orders with regard to us are vague. It is probable that we might pursue our journey without their daring to stop us; but, unfortunately, we have no means of going on, for our beasts are dying. We determine, however, to move on the morrow as far as possible, convinced that the stage will be an exceedingly short one.

February 16.—The envoys return to the charge, and try to convince us that we could not do better than stay where we are. They again ask for our papers, and this time learn our nationality. We send them back without any answer, merely urging them to find a better interpreter of Mongolian, for we cannot understand one another.

We set out on our journey in our best battle-array, with rifles on our shoulders, for the plain swarms with horsemen. It seems as though they had mustered all their warriors—doubtless to frighten us. We enter the pass which rises gently over the ridges, at the bottom of which winds a frozen river. Nothing happens as we cross it, and on the other side we find waiting the envoys whom we had seen the night before. They beg us to remain so as to talk amicably with the Amban, who is on his way from Lhassa, for they have already made preparations to receive him at the bottom of the pass. On the left bank of the frozen river which we are descending, we see numerous black tents, yaks with pack-saddles, and some roomy white canvas tents. We refuse to halt, protesting that we do not understand what they say, as none of them speaks Chinese. Thereupon one of them, the lama, clad in yellow, whose features had already revealed to us his Chinese origin, proceeds immediately to address us in that language. "Stop, I beg of you," he urges; "beyond the pass you will find bitter water, no grass; it is a regular desert. You may believe me; if, however, you doubt my word, I will lend you my horse, and you can assure yourselves that I am speaking the truth."

My first thought was to accept this offer, and ask for two horses, to rejoin our camels which had gone on a little ahead during these negotiations; to order Rachmed to put up tea, sugar, bread, and meat for a week, and then to make with him for Lhassa. But this would have meant leaving our companions in a difficult position, and I quickly abandoned the idea, for this was no time for quitting the helm. At the very moment when these thoughts occurred to me one of our camels fell, never to rise again, and our last horse also fell, so we ordered the vanguard to draw back.

At the same time, escorted by horsemen, and very closely muffled, a mandarin with the blue button comes up, dismounts, and, raising the formidable glasses which shade his eyes, discloses to us a smooth face, intelligent and affable. Our interpreter presents him to us as the Amban himself, who wishes to greet us immediately on his arrival, and asks an audience for the morrow.

He then retires, leaving us to discuss matters with the lama (who speaks Chinese) and his interpreter. The latter is a Mongol, with a fat, jovial, smiling face, with thick lips, beyond which protrudes a very long tooth, giving him when he gapes—and he is always gaping—a good-natured appearance. He assures us that the Amban is a very good fellow, and that we shall be well satisfied when we come to discuss our affairs the next day with him. We try to drag some information out of this interpreter, but he shows remarkable discretion, and our questions only make him leave us quicker than he would otherwise have done. He is evidently restrained by the presence of the Chinese lama, or perhaps he is discreet in obedience to strict orders.

February 17.—Things have not turned out badly, and we still hope to reach Batang. It is a question of committing no blunder, of winning over the natives, of inspiring them with confidence. It is exactly three months since our departure from Tcharkalik, during which time we have lived in a desert, climbed many mountain chains, drunk frozen water, lit fires with dead wood, and shivered under the west wind. And to-day we awake at a height of 17,560 feet. A strong west wind is blowing, and we are just going to drink our tea round our miserable little fire. The only change in our existence is that our advance is checked owing to our want of strength, and also because the object which we have in view is still so very far off that we can never hope to reach it with our own resources; and, therefore, we must get all the help we can from these Thibetans.

Our circumstances certainly leave much to be desired. In the first place, the food is such that the least fastidious appetite wearies of it. Our bill of fare is always the same: meat boiled in mutton fat, tea that never really boils on account of our altitude, and made with water that is sometimes brackish and always dirty, which we get by melting ice that is full of impurities. The frozen meat, too, which we have to chop with an axe, is always tough, and never cooked through, while when we try vegetables or rice, we find it impossible to soften them, and they crackle between our teeth. The dust, mud, and sand that we have swallowed, and the numerous hairs from our furs and beasts, which we find in our food, are things to which we have long ceased to pay any attention, for here we have no longer any pretensions to cleanliness, and we have come to consider even a washing of the hands as a thing of the past. Our cheeks puffed out with the cold, our swollen eyes, our chapped lips, do not differ much in appearance from those of the natives; and presenting such an aspect we cannot make a very good impression upon people who see us for the first time. We must trust to our actions to rectify the erroneous impression which, at first sight, we cannot fail to convey.

But here is someone to announce the Amban. We stretch a clean skin in our men's tent, which is of considerable size, and calmly await the coming of the plenipotentiary from Lhassa. He arrives on foot, accompanied by from fifteen to twenty inferior chiefs of various sizes. Having saluted us politely and with ease, he presents us with the *cata*, the scarf which is the native visiting card, and lays presents at our feet—bands of a cotton stuff called *poulou*, red and yellow and worked with small crosses; then butter in sewn skins, and sacks of *zamba*, i.e. fried barley-meal. We beg him to take a seat in our tent, where-

THE PETTY AMBAN.

upon one of his men lays down a small carpet on which the Amban takes his place. On his right is an old lama, whose head reminds us of a wrinkled apple—beardless, with shaven head, fat, and insignificant, with a rosary in his hand. On his left is the Chinese mandarin, wearing a rich Chinese costume. He has regular features, smooth chin, thick lips, white teeth, swollen eyelids, dark, contracted eyes, with a sly look, and altogether a face that is cunning and sarcastic. Next are drawn up, on the side of the tent which is not reserved for us, various lamas, who crowd together near the entrance, whilst a crowd of servants stand and watch the proceedings. These lamas are of an inferior rank, and have the tanned faces of men who live much in the open. Their features are large, and many of them have a Mongolian cast, with their snub noses, prominent cheek-bones, and small eyes; at all events, they seem to us by no means of pure Thibetan blood.

Their head-dresses are many and various, ranging from the Chinese hat to the Crusader's hooded cloak, the half turban of the date of Charles VII., and monk's hood; we can recognise them all. The cut and colour of their clothes, too, vary, and they wear red, green, yellow, and black. Our tent reminds us of a stage on which the actors are preparing to play *La Tour de Nesle*, with the characters clad in the garments of the Middle Ages. These lamas in their variegated and picturesque costumes do not look ill-disposed, and, as is becoming to "supers," do not breathe a single word, but squat there on their heels, with an air of indifference to what is going on. The leading character is evidently the Amban, a man of moderate size, and quick action. His face is broad and round, his eyes, which are black and of a European cast, have a look of sincerity in them; his lips are thick, his nose straight and broad at the end; his forehead prominent; his hair plaited, and done up in bands like that of European women. Altogether he looks a man of considerable intelligence. He speaks in a hoarse voice, telling his beads with long tapering fingers, and keeping his head bent towards the ground. He pours forth a long tirade in a single breath and a monotonous voice:—" We have orders to stop you wherever we meet you, and to force you to retrace your steps," he first remarks. We reply with a smile that they must not think of making us draw back one single step, for we are sick of these tablelands. As to stopping us, that would be useless, since we have halted here for a conference. But, though tired, we do not want to rest too long, for we are anxious to reach a milder climate.

" Will you go back ? "

" No, no," we reply; " we would rather die. Ask any one of our men whether he would not prefer to die straight off than to go through that fearful journey again."

" We will supply you with all you want for the return."

" It is no good talking of that, for our mind is fully made up. Please, do not reopen the question, for you will only waste your time. Besides, even if we were willing, we could not do so, for without camels we could not manage it, and you have none to give us."

" Where, then, do you want to go ? "

" Merely to rest in some convenient spot, for we are sick and worn out. We have no more horses, our camels are dying, two of our servants are dead, and to force us to stop here would mean death to us."

" After you have rested, where will you go ? "

" We will make for Batang, and, then, striking the Yang-Tse-Kiang, follow it to the sea."

" What is the object of your journey ? "

" Simply to look about, to shoot, and to improve our minds."

" Have you seen the Khan of the Torgots ? "

" No, we have not."

" By what road did you come ? "

" By one that we discovered for ourselves."

"Did you leave your own country long ago?"

"It was summer when we left it last year."

"Are you Russians?"

"No, we are not."

What we say does not seem to convince them. The Amban utters a few words, and someone brings in a packet enveloped in a packing-cloth. From it he produces a box which he opens, and draws out a paper folded like a cravat. This he reads, and then asks for the details of our journey. How many there were at starting, how many horses and camels we had, what arms, our names, and those of our men, etc.

We reply to each question, and the Chinese mandarin writes down our names in a sadly mutilated form. The three envoys then interchange a few words, after which the Amban, taking the sheet again, says, "Here is an order which I received two months ago from Pekin. It is an order to stop the Russians, Pètsou * of Petsokou arriving with Lobolou and thirty men." (Then followed a list of camels, guns, etc.) "You are neither Pètsou nor Lobolou, for the names which you have given us do not in the least resemble these. Written information has reached us that Niklaï (Nicolas Prjevalsky) is dead, and that Pètsou has taken command of the men whom he had got together so as to reach Lhassa. We have also been told that other Russians,† less numerous, are travelling in the district of the Koukou Nor, and that they are possibly making for Lhassa by the Tsaïdam road. Are you these Russians?"

"We are not Russians at all."

"Then you are Palan (*i.e.* English)?"

"No."

"You must know that the English are the enemies of our people, many of whom they have killed with their far-carrying

---

* Pevtzoff, of St. Petersburg, and Roborovsky.

† The brothers Grum Grjimaïlo.

guns, and our people do not want the English to penetrate into Thibet at any price."

"No, we are not English, we are French."

As, however, our Mongolian interpreter renders "French" by "Tarang" and then translates "Tarang" into Thibetan by "Palan," the Amban believes us to acknowledge that we are English—a contradiction that he cannot understand. The only means by which we can explain our nationality is to use the Chinese expression whilst addressing the lama who speaks this language, consequently we say to him, "We are ta fa kić" *i.e.* Frenchmen.

The lama who acts as secretary, thereupon makes a short explanation in Thibetan to his chief, who finishes by understanding that we are a distinct people from the English, and excuses himself for his mistake in these words, "Never having seen any Frenchmen before, we could not, of course, recognise them. However, allow me to withdraw now, so that I may consult with my chiefs; to-morrow you shall have an answer."

Such, in brief, was our first conversation, which had lasted several hours, through the necessity of having two interpreters. Besides, these men would not trust us, and laid traps for us, repeating questions that we had already answered, and returning suddenly to a point that seemed settled, so as to assure themselves that our story did not vary. The conversation was interspersed with cups of tea, drunk out of the most beautiful Chinese ware, while the Amban's cup was of green jade. Having caught cold on the journey here, they were continually coughing, and using their handkerchiefs, made of a cotton stuff (*poulou*) sewn in the shape of the cover of a book, which they open and shut just as if it were an actual book, and place in their bosoms. They repeatedly, too, took snuff, which is a white powder, sometimes carried in a flat bottle with a scoop attached to the cork. In other cases it is shaken out of a cylindrical metal box, which has a cover closing by means of a pin. Depositing the snuff on the thumb-nail, they sniff it up with great satisfaction, and then pass the box on to their neighbours.

At last, however, the list of our little troop was completed, but the lama, who had ticked us off on his rosary, made us out to be eleven instead of twelve, because Parpa had been forgotten, with the result that the whole process of enumerating and reading out our names had to be gone through again, while he again ticked them off. All these operations were performed very leisurely and steadily, as befits men of high rank who have plenty of time to lose, so that this first conference lasted about five hours.

The Amban will now write and tell his superiors what account we have given of ourselves, and they will then inform him what line of conduct he is to pursue. Meanwhile, he will supply us with provisions, for we do not want to use up the small supply we have. To do that would place us entirely in their hands, and we are quite in the dark as to what the future has in store for us. We mean, therefore, to live on the sheep and meal with which they will supply us.

February 20.—We employ the time we have to spend in the pass of Dam, by studying the Thibetans of high degree and the lamas. We begin with a festival, for this is their New Year's Day, and they keep up the feast for five days more. Early in the morning the interpreter came to invite us to the Amban's tent to celebrate the day with him. This fine old Mongol had put on a sort of red hood for the occasion, and had evidently been drinking; for his eyes were more brilliant than they generally are, and, besides, he emits an odour of arrack, which at once proclaims the reason of his good-humour and beaming smile. "Come," said he, "come at once. It is the first day of the new year, and the Amban is impatient to see you. He has prepared a feast, too, for you, so come directly."

We at once make our way down towards their camp, which lies

below ours on the other side of the ice; numerous black tents surrounding the white ones which the Amban and the chiefs occupy. There is a perpetual coming and going of servants, who are assisted by the savage inhabitants of the tableland, whose right arms, in spite of the severity of the weather, are outside their tunics, while half their body appears completely bare. It is they who gather the *argol*, search for ice, cut up the animals they kill, look after the saddle-horses, mules, and yaks, and keep the fire burning by means of a skin in which they very cleverly confine the air, which is then forced out through an iron tube plunged in the heap of *argol*. The tents form a pretty picture, reminding one of a bedecked fleet, as the garlands of prayers, running from top to top, wave in the breeze. The camp itself is all alive with men, while the mountain sides swarm with yaks, which have brought the provisions for the hundred or two hundred souls who are honouring us with their presence. In front of the Amban's tent is an open one which does duty as kitchen, and near it we perceive a man who looks as though he were making butter in a jar, but he is really mixing it in the tea.

The Amban himself, who is awaiting us in front of his tent, sends some servants to help us over the ice, which they do by holding us up by the arms, for we are guests of no small consequence. We mount the bank, along the bottom of which great care is necessary in walking, and the Amban advances to meet us with a smile that stretches right across his smooth round face.

At his request we precede him into his tent, which is a four-sided one with a square sloping roof. As the Amban is a layman, a servant with long hair, hanging in a plait, lifts the curtain as we enter. The Amban invites us to take our seats on a sort of daïs to the right of the entrance, a second one, a little higher than ours, being reserved for him at the other end. He sits on it, cross-legged, on a tiger-skin, with cushions at his back, some of them covered with Chinese silk, and others, if I mistake not, with Indian muslin.

We wish him a happy new year and good health, not forgetting to add, as is our way in Champagne, "and Paradise afterwards," a formula, which, to satisfy a believer in the transmigra-

TENT OF THE ENVOYS FROM LHASSA.

tion of souls, is rendered, "We wish you a still better place after death." He thanks us profusely, and expresses his pleasure that we should have met for their greatest *fête*, adding, "This is a good omen, for those who pass New Year's Day together become good friends."

"We have no doubt on this point, for, as a matter of fact, we have no ill-feeling towards you. We look upon you as an honourable man, with whom we would gladly be good friends." And so on for about twenty minutes, as is the custom in the East—a custom which we may compare with the salute of two swordsmen before beginning the combat.

Then we ask him when the reply of his superiors will come.

"Very soon," he said.

"We should take it as a great favour if you would let us know what you mean by this expression 'very soon,' for in some countries it means 'in an hour,' in others 'in a day' or 'in a year.' What does it mean with you?"

The Mongolian interpreter seemed more than ever under the influence of arrack, so loud was his laugh, and when the words were translated to him, the Amban laughed too. "It is quite true," he replied, "that there ought not to be any misunderstanding about the meaning of words, and I may tell you that 'very soon' means in this case 'in about six days,' for our chiefs will doubtless want to consult the Chinese mandarin. He is not in Lhassa, but lives at two days' journey west of that town. I am very sorry for this delay, but it cannot be helped."

Meanwhile the chief of the lamas who are here enters the tent, and takes his seat on the left-hand side of the Amban on the same daïs. Before them stands a small table bearing their teacups with silver lids, into which some young men are constantly pouring the mixture of tea and butter from earthenware teapots. One of them has evidently snatched the teapot out of the hands of a comrade who wishes to prevent him from coming into the tent, and is holding him back by the skirt of his robe. In order to free himself, he is kicking violently backwards, whilst lifting the curtain, with a beaming smile on his face.

We remained a long time with the Amban drinking his tea and butter, which he was incessantly offering us, together with sweetmeats, consisting of pastry and queer-looking objects, which we all liked, though they were not particularly attractive to the eye. I must, however, mention some nuts preserved in sugar.

The conversation flagged but little, turning all the time on our situation. We complained of our forced stay here, and of our not being allowed to enjoy a much-needed rest, and said we failed to understand this fashion of receiving strangers. To this the Amban replied that he was merely obeying orders, that no one wished us ill, that their customs were different from ours, and that in a very few days, after the *fête* was over, everything would be arranged in accordance with our wishes.

The first thing that strikes us in examining the tent is the quantity of sacred objects in every corner. Around the centre pole, which supports the roof, twines, like ivy, a cluster of little niches, like those in which the Orthodox place their sacred pictures. To the left of the Amban an altar has been reared upon some chests, on the top of which is an image of Buddha, enclosed in a gilded case; in front is a line of seven little copper cups containing saffron and oil; a light is glimmering, and perfumes are burning in a box, whilst odoriferous sticks, placed in teapots, are smouldering away; on the two steps of the altar stand some little figures, cut in butter, amongst which I can distinguish a sheep's head without horns, having on the forehead protuberances of white sugar, some small columns of the same material, and, in saucers, pieces of confectionery offered as a sacrifice to the divinity.

After having drunk a great many cups of tea, we express a wish to retire, whereupon the Amban, supported by the chief lama, reiterates once more what he had already repeated a score of times. "Let us try and arrange the business we have in hand," he urges, "don't let us disagree," and, so saying, he presses together the inside of his thumbs, and, insisting on our friendship, makes use of this comparison: "Two beautiful porcelain cups placed together on a table look very well. But knock them together and they break to pieces. Don't let us clash, don't let us clash," he repeats, as he rises to show us the way out. As we go out everyone salutes us with a smile, and it is easy to see that their orders are not to give us needless offence. Just as we start, a flourish of trumpets is heard above us, and, lifting our eyes, we perceive huge garlands fluttering on the summit of the perpendicular granite rocks which overhang the left of the camp. These garlands consist of yaks' tails interspersed between pieces of coloured stuffs imprinted with prayers. Near them are seated some lamas holding trumpets, from which proceed excruciating sounds that rend the air and are re-echoed on the mountains. When they are not blowing these instruments, they are chanting prayers in a rhythmic cadence, forming a chorus in which deep bass voices support shrill trebles.

Under pretext of taking a walk, we direct our steps towards a black tent which has quite recently been pitched in the roadway of the pass above our camp. We see squatted round a fire eight long-haired men under the command of a shorn lama. They are conversing quietly, and smoking a little pipe formed of an earthenware bowl and a bone stem, which they hand round to each other in turn. These are the poor wretches whose work it is to gather the *argol*, and who have no part in the New Year's celebrations. What we took for a tent in the distance is really only half a tent, a mere shelter of black sack-cloth, open on the side from which there is no wind. They sleep there on a heap of straw and chips; in a corner stand their bows and lances, and in the middle three stones form a fireplace for use on windy days. Their simple dress is cut out of sheep-skins, frayed at the lower extremities, full of holes, and extraordinarily dirty. Their faces, blackened with grease and smoke, suggest the lowest type of savage that one can imagine. On looking at their narrow heads we ask ourselves what brains they can possibly contain, and are by no means astonished at the unusual authority which the lamas exercise over beings so wanting in intelligence, so little capable of any exercise of will, whose sensations cannot differ much from those of their yaks and dogs. Let us hope that all the Thibetans do not resemble this band of animals with human faces.

We leave them to regale ourselves on a sheep's head that has been cooked under the *argol* on the fire, just as we roast potatoes in the ashes, and excellent it is. Travellers on the steppes often cook their meat in this way, because there is no flame or smoke to betray them.

So draws to its close the first day of the Thibetan year, and as we wrap ourselves in our blankets the lamas recommence their prayers, and are still chanting as we fall asleep.

February 21.—In continuation of the festival, the trumpets resound on the top of the cliffs, there is singing in the camp, and the garlands of prayers are waving in the west wind. The first event of the day is a visit from another interpreter, a Mongolian lama, a native of Ourga, a town lying in Chinese Mongolia, not far from the frontiers of Siberia. He is of moderate height, very alert, very vigorous, and a big liar, as he soon proves, when he explains that he comes from Lhassa, and that, having lost his way, he "chanced" to find himself at the spot where we had buried Imatch. He had probably been sent to make sure of Imatch's nationality, for we had returned him as a Kalmuck, and, if he has examined him at close quarters, he will certainly have taken him for such, for poor Imatch had the very small nose and the ugliness of that race. The new interpreter examines our men, and declares them to be natives of North Turkestan. Then, without losing a moment, he proceeds to insinuate that he would be very thankful for the gift of a revolver.

February 22.—To-day the Mongolian interpreter makes a confidant of poor silly Abdullah, telling him that if he (the interpreter) remains here it will only be because he has no money wherewith to return home. He makes out that he arrived here some time before with a caravan of pilgrims, that he then fell ill and was obliged to stop here, but that he is ever thinking of his home at Ourga; throwing himself on our generosity to help him. Although we do not place too much faith in his story, it seems to us at least probable, for accidents of this sort must often happen in Thibet, just as they were formerly of not unfrequent occurrence in the Holy Land. In vain do we "pump" him for information with respect to ourselves; he either knows nothing, or will say nothing.

March 1.—Since the 21st of February we have received visits from the smaller chiefs, who sometimes brought us little presents, and also accepted with pleasure gifts of sugar, and especially of raisins, of which they are very fond. They have passed a good deal of time in our men's tents, examining our arms, and listening gladly to the rather unmelodious notes of an accordion. Every now and then they would suddenly put a question to us, evidently trying to catch us contradicting ourselves, and then, with unheard-of patience, would sit waiting for an opportunity to beg, in the most natural manner possible, for an explanation which we had already given. All the time they observed us narrowly, though they were very polite, as is their way. We might find considerable amusement in watching the manner in which they transact their business, were it not that many of our men are ill; some are suffering from sickness, others from diarrhœa, the latter, we think, being caused by the water we drink, which is drawn from under the ice, at the source of the river which flows down to Lake Namtso. The cold is certainly less keen, the minimum varying between 4° and 9° below zero, but we suffer exceedingly from the north-west winds. All our camels, too, are dying one after the other, without any apparent malady; they are simply used up. Their dead bodies attract numerous lammergeiers, some of which we bring down. One of them emits a strong odour of musk, and Parpa hastens to remove its fat. The lama from Ourga begs us to give him the bodies, so that he may cut out certain portions of them, the liver amongst others, in order to make medicines of them. But being a lama, he does this work by night, for fear of being seen by the savages, as it is, it seems unbecoming his rank for him to do such things.

Laden yaks arrive almost daily, sometimes by night, from the south; so we conclude that more people are coming to Dam, which is the name of the spot where we are. On the 28th ult. the interpreters assured us that the answer would soon be here, and begged us not to lose patience. The same day the Amban, accompanied by the principal lamas, went on an excursion—scaling the heights which border the pass, so as to catch a glimpse of Lake Namtso, which he had never seen. This fact proves that the inhabitants of Lhassa do not often travel out of their own district, or that they do not care for exercise of this kind, however conducive to health it may be. At all events, the Namtso is supposed to be the largest piece of water in Thibet, and is regarded as sacred, under the name of "Heavenly Lake," and yet here are civil and religious personages who have never taken the trouble to come and see it.

March 2.—Yesterday morning early the sky was overcast, and when the storm burst, the valley disappeared in the dust. All night it blew a gale, and several tents belonging to the Thibetans were carried away in a squall, but we were all right in ours, which is a fourfold one, for the Amban had given us a beautiful double tent, which we had thrown over ours, so that, besides the extra thickness, there is room between them in which to store various articles, and also for an entrance hall. The whole is strengthened by huge stones, with the result that it defies the wind. The minimum temperature last night was 10° below zero, and several of us complained on waking of headache—the usual effect of mountain storms, even if they occur when one is asleep. Towards midday a snow-cloud passed over us, and a strong north-west wind was blowing, a very different thing from the west wind which comes up across the Namtso, rushing through the pass. In the afternoon our long-toothed friend brought us a little milk, which we had been asking for to give our invalids, and at the same time he informed us that the great chiefs would soon be here. We had suspected this from the early morning, for numerous yaks, with loads, had arrived during the night, and we had seen men, with great difficulty, pitching a large tent, and had been amused to see a strong gust of wind carrying off the canvas. The perpetual coming and going of men, the general commotion, and the fact of the lesser chiefs superintending the work, had aroused our suspicions, which the indiscretion of the interpreter had only served to confirm. So, when he had left us, we took up our position at a suitable spot with our glasses, and fixed our eyes on the descent of the pass.

First, pack-horses, well harnessed, having on their necks tinkling bells, or tufts of red (the colour denoting authority) come in sight; then horsemen, well attired, who lose their way amidst the bogs, not seeming to know the path made below the ridges, which is reached by a detour. Some long-haired savages shout to them, others hasten to meet them, take their bridles and help their beasts over the ice, while on their arrival in camp, the occupants of all the tents rush out and surround them. They, however, form but the vanguard; and the camp is now filled with excitement, and servants set out in the direction of the pass.

It is not long before we catch sight of the great chiefs mounted on quick, surefooted horses, which drag along the men who are holding on to their bridles as if to lead them. We make out three important personages amongst the crowd. Covered with furs lined with yellow silk, they look so fat and enormous that we wonder they do not crush their agile little horses. On their heads they wear the feathered hats of the Chinese mandarins, but over a hood which covers their neck and face, of which absolutely nothing is visible, for their eyes are protected by prominent glasses, which again, as an additional precaution, are overhung by a visor. Behind them, with a great noise of bells, trots a large escort in varied costumes. Though this spectacle presents a certain amount of pomp, it seems to us ridiculous.

In the camp all the civil and religious chiefs stand in a row awaiting the mandarins, and when the latter arrive, the chiefs make a deep bow, remaining where they stood. The Amban alone approaches the visitors, and congratulates two of them with whom he shakes hands. Then, without dismounting, they go to their appointed tents, the crowd disperses, and everybody returns to his work. When we reflect that all these people are gathered here because of us, we realise that they are paying us a high compliment.

Meanwhile, however, a little drama is being enacted in our camp. The Dungan's camel had been for two days uttering plaintive groans, and now to-day, just two months before her time of sixteen months has expired, she gives birth to a dead calf. The poor mother licks and smells it, hanging over it and crying plaintively. Timour is very sorry at its death, for, he said, "The little thing had humps enough to become a perfect camel."

Then the interpreters come up, and ask us to grant an audience to the great men who had just arrived. We reply that we shall be very happy to receive them at once. When our answer has been transmitted, quite a large band makes its way to our tent, preceded by two individuals who are sumptuously attired in the Chinese style. These two approach arm in arm, and one of them, small, short, round, and bent in the back, leans heavily on his companion's arm. With a venerable air these two approach slowly, stopping to take breath every fifteen steps. Perhaps this mode of progression is meant to be in good form, to impress us, and give us plenty of time to go politely and meet them. But we are rude enough to remain in our tent, and only go out of it when they have got on to our ground. We then exchange salutations with the two chiefs, who are introduced to us as the Ta-Lama and the Ta-Amban, after which some porters deposit at our feet five sacks—one of rice, one of *zamba*, one of meal, one of Chinese

THIBETANS LOADING A YAK (p. 64).

peas, and one of butter. Then we invite the two ambassadors to enter our tent, where skins are spread ready for them. The simplicity of our furniture is evidently a surprise to them, for they appear to hesitate, and make difficulties before entering. When once they have entered, they ask permission to sit on their own little rugs, and their servants lay down for one of them a wild cat's skin, and for the other a small mattress lined with silk. They apologise for these precautions on the score of their age and fatigue.

The three who had been the first to enter into negotiations with us take their seats near them, in front of us, and the conversation commences. At first it consists only of small civilities.

"How are you?" said the Ta-Lama.

"Not at all well, for this is a wretched place."

This answer rather disconcerts them; they had evidently expected greater amiability from us, and our old acquaintance, the Amban, hangs his head, for he had represented us as well-mannered people. We ask them, in our turn, whether they have had a pleasant journey.

"Yes, although the road is a bad one. We had to travel by easy stages on account of our age. The festival of the New Year, too, has delayed us; otherwise you would have seen us much sooner. This festival we are obliged to keep in compliance with our religion."

Then come questions about ourselves, and the object of our travels, to which we make the same reply as we have already made at least twenty times to their subordinate, the Amban, while they repeat his proposals.

"You will now retrace your steps."

"No, that is impossible."

"If you will, we will supply you with all that you want. This is the best course for you to pursue, and we shall part good friends. Think over my suggestion, which I advise you to accept; I venture to hope that we shall not fall out, for we have come without any soldiers, though we might have brought some from Lhassa. That proves our good intentions."

"It is quite useless to propose that we should return, and to advise us to reflect, for we do not speak without having already reflected. We have come from the West, urged on by fate, by a force which has carried us across deserts by a road which you yourselves do not know. Our aim is to go to Batang and then to Tonquin, there to rejoin our fellow-countrymen, who are living on land which we have taken from the Emperor of China. You are powerless against our resolution, and you may rely upon it that we will not take one single step northwards. You do not frighten us in the least, for we have come from the end of the world without being stopped, and we shall now pursue our way onwards, and you will help us. It is for you rather than for us to reflect, and you will see that Buddha himself wills it thus. We would rather die than return. That is our last word."

As the sun is now setting they rise to leave us, evidently put out at our having so expressed ourselves before their escort. They bid us farewell, and before they have gone very far, wishing to have the last word, the Ta-Lama repeats "Reflect, reflect."

To which I reply in French, very disrespectfully, "All right, old fellow." (Oui, mon vieux!)

"What does he say?"

"He is merely saying 'Good night' in his own language," replies Abdullah.

The two great chiefs then departed, while we remained to fight the question out with the Amban and the two others with whom we had previously been dealing. The Amban who, as we begin to believe, has taken a fancy to us, was very vexed.

"Whatever made you speak like that to my chiefs? Remember that they are the two first men at Lhassa, and have as much power as the Ministers. Do be more amiable to-morrow. Tell me what you want, and I will talk to them accordingly. Only do not change your minds meanwhile, for if you contradict me, they will accuse me of having sold myself to you, and of having espoused your interests, and even tried to get for you more than you ask for."

"Our wish is to go to Batang. You will furnish us with the means of transport and provisions, and we will pay for them. That is what we want to-day, and what we shall not cease to want until we obtain it."

"I will mention it to my chiefs, but can insist on nothing, for if I did they would only distrust me, and lay an information against me, with the result that I should be cruelly punished."

With these words they leave, and we go to warm ourselves at the fire, and confide to one another the impressions which the two ambassadors have made on us. They are so unlike that they seem as though they had been created to present a striking antithesis. The Ta-Lama is thin and nervous, with the small dark eyes of a European, very bright and very straight; his nose is pointed, and a prominent chin is made to appear still longer, owing to a plaited tuft of hair that is twisted in the shape of a rat's tail. His face has a wary look, and a smile which might be either benevolent or ironical, but seems rather Mephistophelian. When he smiles he shows his white teeth, and he speaks at a rapid rate and in a monotonous voice, as though he were repeating a litany. His indifferent attitude shows that he attaches no importance whatever to his own words; but his eyes are for ever busy in examining us. He affects utter unconcern, but all the time betrays his preoccupation of mind by the way in which, with dry, thin hands, and long nails, like a falcon's claws, he tells his beads.

The Ta-Amban, on the contrary, is a fat man, with a broad,

long face, and enormous head, while the general appearance of his body, which looks like a big jar, might be indicated by four ovals, the smallest of which would stand for his head, the largest for his body, and the two others for his legs. His arms are short, and look more like fins, his hands are plump with small fingers, his chin is round and double, his cheeks are pendulous, and his eyes are contracted and shapeless. You would think him good-natured were it not for his suspicious look. He speaks with animation in a full round voice, smiting his knee with his hand, and evidently has Chinese blood in his veins.

Concerning the Ta-Lama, we all agree that he is clever, cunning, and intelligent; as to the Ta-Amban, he seems less intelligent, but more stubborn.

We sit up till late, talking in the moonlight, and can hear Abdullah and the Dungan reciting their prayers within the latter's tent, a sign that the outlook seems dark to them, for it is only when things appear bad that they address themselves to Heaven. The sleep of the rest of our band, too, has been somewhat curtailed by the events of the day. Something new has happened, and that is enough to excite them and keep them awake.

Iça, Rachmed, Parpa, and Timour are seated cross-legged in the entrance of their tent, near their fire, which flickers like a will-o'-the-wisp, and the moon is shedding her pale light on the mountain, making it look smaller and flatter, and the vault of heaven all the deeper. Timour is gazing quietly and thoughtfully up to the sky.

"What are you looking at, Timour? Is it the moon?" I ask.

"No, the Bear."

"What are you watching it for?"

"I am glad to see it there, for there will be plenty of grass for the herds, when the Bear is low in the sky after sunset."

Rachmed, who is out of sorts and in a bad humour, interrupts—

" Show me the Bear."

" There it is," said Timour, stretching his hand in the direction of sparkling Orion.

" That is not the Bear," says Rachmed, " that is the Balance. You don't know what you are talking about. You had better keep your mouth shut than talk such nonsense. How can the Balance have any effect upon the grass? If it is a rainy season, or if we have had a great deal of snow in winter, then there is plenty of grass, but the stars have nothing to do with it. You talk for the pleasure of talking. You are a real latter-day Mussulman, a regular donkey," etc. He then rails at Islam in general, reproaching it with being stupid and irrational, and, his wrath increasing with his words, exclaims, " You donkey! you donkey!"

And poor Timour, abashed by this eloquence, can only repeat plaintively and suppliantly—" Rachmed *aga!* Rachmed *aga!*" (" Rachmed, my elder brother, my elder brother ").

Rachmed ceases his reproaches, but on hearing the Dungan's and Abdullah's prayers his wrath bursts out again. " Listen, too, to those donkeys, who have faith only when they are afraid. Ah! there are no more real Mussulmans, none."

Then the wind rises, and so draws upon itself the maledictions which were going to fall once more on poor Timour, who was still appealing to Rachmed as " my elder brother, my elder brother," which is a Turk's most affectionate term. Timour is very fond of Rachmed, who likes him in return.

Such little scenes as this are our only distraction.

March 3.—We confer with the two great chiefs, and, after many quarrels and reconciliations, at last convince them that we are neither English nor Russian, but French, and to our great joy extract from them permission to move on.

March 7.—This morning the sun is shining brightly, and the snow that fell on the preceding days stands out resplendent and dazzling on the mountain. It is grand weather for our departure, though it is not a final move, for we are only going to instal ourselves in a better place, there to wait again.

The camp is all astir: on all sides are men running after their beasts, collecting them, driving them on with shrill whistles, and swinging their slings. As the long plaits of hair would be in the way when the Thibetans stoop, they twist them round their heads.

They have great difficulty in catching their beasts, especially to-day, when the yaks are frightened by our camels. It is only after more than one fruitless attempt that they will allow themselves to be caught by the horn, to which is tied the cord that is attached to the ring in the muffle. Their masters have to approach them very carefully, and can only seize them by surprise. Loading them is a still more difficult business; and it takes a tremendous time to fasten our chests on to their backs. But the patience of these men is endless, and they always finish by mastering the animal; for as soon as they have got hold of it, they hopple it and load it, in spite of heels and horns, but never beat it.

These Thibetans are very quick over their work. Each time they raise a heavy load they force out the air from their lungs by a vigorous hiss. They handle great weights with considerable ease, for their arms, though not very muscular, are tough, and set in solid shoulders, which are supported by deep necks, and the length of the forearm is remarkable. Lamas, stick in hand, give their orders, and reprimand them; but these savages do their work cheerfully, and are very obedient and respectful to the lamas, to whom they listen in the most humble posture, with backs bent and hanging tongue.

We have had some small Thibetan horses given us which are

THE CARAVAN IN MOTION.

full of go, and which feed on raw flesh, as we have seen with our own eyes. These carnivorous beasts have marvellous legs, and are as clever as acrobats; they balance themselves with the greatest care on the ice or amid dirty bogs, and then, gaining the path with a bound, carry us along at a rapid trot, to which we have long been unaccustomed. Anyone would imagine that they find us to be as light as feathers, and we certainly look far more like lean hermits than fat monks.

We soon rejoined a caravan that started before we did. The loaded yaks go along in utter disorder, their drivers letting them stop at will to eat a root, to sniff pieces of *argol*, perhaps to reflect. In three and a half hours we rode nearly fourteen miles, up hill and down dale, but more often the latter, for we were to encamp near a frozen river which empties its waters into the Namtso.

Our old friend the Amban welcomed us to his tent, where a delicious repast awaited us, consisting of a yak's tongue smoked, and, by way of vegetables, preserved salted carrots, and red and green pepper; then some cakes of unleavened bread, and as much tea and butter as we could drink. Our excellent host admired our appetite, and kept urging us to satisfy it to the full.

Between our camp and that of the chiefs from Lhassa are pitched the tents of some nomads who are driving their herds this way. They are, it seems, inscribed among the subjects of China, and pay taxes as such, " but in all other respects," says the Amban, " they obey us; their tribe is that of the Djashas. In summer they disperse over the tableland of the north."

When we passed by their tents, they came out to salute us, and we recognised their chief, a big toothless fellow, whom we had come across before reaching the Namtso. He strikes us as a half-bred Chinaman. To-day he wears a sort of uniform, consisting of a jacket with a red collar and adorned with copper buttons bearing the numbers of English regiments in India. These buttons are of no earthly use to him, for they have no corresponding buttonholes, but they are the sign of wealth, the proof of a high position, just because they are not actually wanted. The superfluous is reserved for the powerful of the earth.

The Amban begged us to remain in his tent until ours was ready; but when we told him that we should like a walk because we were cold, he led us back to our camp, saying, "Our customs forbid me to leave my guests before a shelter is ready for them. I will therefore accompany you." We took advantage of this custom to ask him one or two questions—first, the name of the splendid chain from which rise Huc and Gabet, each this evening having its summit in a turban of clouds, reminding one of Persia and the well-known turban of the Demavend. This chain, he tells us, is called Samda Kansain; and the river, which flows close by, Samda Tchou, borrowing its name from the mountain which feeds it.

Then we talked to him about the *serou* (unicorn), of whose existence Father Huc had been assured, and he told us that this animal lives in the Ghoorkas' country, in India, and that it has one horn, not on the top of the head, but on the nose, so that he was evidently describing the rhinoceros.

Before sunset we perceived at an enormous height a large flock of birds, which we took to be geese, making north. Very welcome was the sight of them, for they seemed to be harbingers of the spring. Timour, too, was persuaded that the warm weather was really coming, for he had seen a fresh blade of grass; and, to prove his words, he got up, examined the bottom of the mountain, and soon returned with a blade, which he held solemnly in his hand, and contemplated with glad eyes—for Timour is a poet, a true lover of Nature. Then to bed, to dream of home, for the gentle west wind produces on this bare plain the same murmurs, the same plaintive sounds, as in our native woods.

March 8.—The west wind is still blowing, and snow falls at intervals. The sun appears and disappears. Then the wind increases, the heavens are darkened, and the cold, after the warmth of the afternoon, is simply insupportable. In spite of the weather, however, the Amban pays us a visit, and again exhorts us to be patient, for it will take time to get ready at Lhassa all the things which we require. Before quitting Dam they had drawn up, at our dictation, a long list of our requirements—clothes of all sorts, shoes, hats, skin, large and small cymbals, and even prayers and objects of worship. They had promised, too, to procure some horses, and to send them on here quickly. But the Amban is afraid that we may lose patience, for he cannot help noticing the hurry we are all in to start, not a single one of us having the least wish to stop here. The Amban insists on the purity of his intentions. "We look upon you as brothers, and our wish is to be as agreeable as possible to you; and if we keep you here, it is only because we must await letters from our superiors at Lhassa, who are satisfied of your honesty. But then our ways are not like yours. We never hurry in business matters. There is a council which decides all important matters, and you know that the members of a numerous council do not immediately agree. If it depended only on me, you should at once have all that you want; but you see that, even here, we are three great chiefs and about twenty smaller ones. The one mistrusts the other, and it needs great prudence not to lay oneself open to accusation." This fear of an accusation—which the Amban has mentioned on previous occasions—proves that Lhassa is a hotbed of intrigue, power being divided and much sought after, and that those who possess it guard it very jealously.

Our guest next asks for information regarding our customs and manners, the position of women in our country and their looks; and then he speaks of the books of the English, and of the astonishing inventions which they have brought to India, though he himself had never seen them. He expresses his astonishment that we should take the trouble to travel, "for," said he, "what is the good of visiting distant lands when you can spend your life in reading about them without leaving home? I, at all events, have not the slightest wish ever to travel outside Thibet, for my curiosity is quite satisfied by our religious books."

THE COOKING TENT.

CHAPTER XI.

PRESENTS FROM LHASSA.

Breakfasting with the Ta-Amban and Ta-Lama—Diplomatic Indignation—Two Barbarian Petty Chiefs—An Effectual Call to Order—A Sunset Scene—Feasting on a Sheep's Head—A "Dainty Dish"—At Soubrou—Resting at Di-Ti—Water-Carriers—An *Entente Cordiale*—Characteristics and Habits of the Natives of the Di-Ti Country—A Specimen of Primeval Man—Nigan: Another Stoppage—The Talai-Lama's Presents: Sacred Objects—Return Presents—A Lama-Guide—The Ta-Amban's Advice—A Pet Ram—Timour, Parpa, and Iça Go Back.

CHIEF OF THE DJASHAS.

March 14.—We are invited to meet the Ta-Amban and the Amban at breakfast in the tent of the Ta-Lama, who has a most sumptuous repast ready for us. It lasts four hours, during which time we plunge our chopsticks into some thirty very rich dishes that must have cost a great deal, for it is by no means easy in Thibet to procure young palm-shoots, dates from India, peaches from Leh (Lada), jujubes from Batang, berries from Landjou, edible seaweed and shell-fish from the coast, etc. etc. Out of all these different productions of the Asiatic *cuisine* a few are decidedly eatable, and we confine ourselves to them; but what we prefer to everything else is the plentiful supply of hot milk, in which we dip our dates so as to thaw them. Their idea, perhaps, was to win us over by such a splendid feast, but we remain as firm as ever when, after the tables have been removed and negotiations reopened, they beg us to wait yet a little longer. Our indignation bursts out anew, and we rise at once without listening to any more circumlocution. They are astonished at our departure; but when they see us thrashing our interpreter, who has been making signs to them behind our backs, they understand that our patience is exhausted. The result of this interrupted feast is the extraction of a promise that we shall make our way forward.

March 16.—We discuss the route that we shall follow. The chiefs undertake to show us the road to Batang; only the stages are to be short, in order that the couriers expected from Lhassa may join us the sooner. Amidst falling snow, after a minimum temperature of 13° below zero, we begin our preparations for departure.

The place where we are to await the couriers is called Di-Ti, which the Amban represents as a sort of Paradise in comparison with our present location, which is rendered uninhabitable by the incessant west wind. It seems that "down there" we shall find grass, brushwood, juniper-trees, corn and moderate heat; for we shall be on much lower ground; here we are at an altitude of 16,170 feet. We beg the Amban to be good enough to tell us where Di-Ti is; but he answers that he does not know exactly, and sends for two petty barbarian chieftains, whom he questions in our presence. They enter, bent double, out of deference to their superior, and with tongues hanging out of their mouths, like greyhounds in summer after chasing a hare.

"Do you know Di-Ti?"

"Yes, we are driving our herds there."

"Is it a nice place?"

"Yes."

"In what direction is it?"

"In that." (They point north-east.)

"Is it far?"

"No."

"How many *lavère* off is it?" (*Lavère* corresponds in Thibet to *li* in China, being about a quarter of a mile.)

Lavère, lavère, lavère, murmur the two savages, looking at each other, and scratching their ears; "we do not know their country," taking it for the name of a camp—a mistake that is, after all, intelligible on the part of savages, who have no need of precision, though we laugh at it none the less. The Amban therefore dismisses them, and they withdraw with deep reverences, thumbs raised, and tongues still hanging out.

The lamas then set about obtaining from the Djashas yaks and horses enough for the whole caravan. So many are required that the Djashas—or Djashougs, Tatshougs, Ttashougs, for we hear the name pronounced in all these different ways—refuse to supply us, and, getting angry, shout and threaten. Then the Ta-Lama summons their chiefs, who immediately on receiving the order appear, calm but crestfallen. The Ta-Lama bids his servants throw open the front of his tent, and from his daïs—where he remains sitting cross-legged, his hands in his sleeves—talks quietly to them. He has scarcely opened his mouth when the savages bend, and, in the posture of a schoolboy awaiting a swishing, lower their heads, scarcely daring to raise their eyes, and cry humbly—

"*Lalesse, lalesse!*" (We are ready.)

And when the Ta-Lama, in conclusion, says to them, still in his quiet tones—

"Is it possible that you would displease the Djongoro Boutchi" (the living Buddha) "and the Ta-Lama" (Great Lama)?—

"No," they reply, groaning and falling on their knees.

"Very well; then obey."

"*Lalesse, lalesse!* It is all right."

A servant thereupon bids them retire, which they do backwards, in the respectful attitude of the country. The tent is again closed, and the chiefs draw themselves up, and quite good-humouredly return to their own tents.

Convinced that we are now really about to start, I spend a few moments in admiring the scene, and am straightway lost in ecstasy before a scene which Messrs. Cook can promise to their clients when, in years to come, they have organised trips to Thibet. To describe it, however, would take another pen than mine. I can but gaze thoughtfully, as do the shepherds on the tablelands, at the splendid chain of the Ningling Tangla, as its snow-capped peaks are lost in the gold of the sunset. The light vaporous atmosphere is, so to speak, saturated with this golden light; while behind us the Samda-Kansain lies bathed in violet tints, and above it are clustered thick snow-clouds, through which, rent by the wind, are seen here and there patches of blue sky.

March 18.—We start in a north-easterly direction. The weather is splendid, but the reflection of the sun on the snow literally scorches our faces and eyes. We learn on the road that between here and Tatsien-lou there are eighty more or less difficult passes. It is the interpreter with the long tooth who tells me that he once counted them when going to Lhassa by this route; he also informs us that there are very few spots in Thibet where it is possible to grow a little wheat, though they have good crops of barley. The other cereals, including rice, are imported from India. At night we encamp in a valley at Tashé-Roua, which means, in the language of the steppes, the "Gathering of Tents at Tashé," though we had seen only three or four tents on the whole stage, in the mouths of gorges, near the ice.

Besides lending us some yak-drivers, our friends have also provided us with two men whose business it is to collect fuel for our fires. This evening they arrive with their gleanings in a sack, which they empty at the entrance of our servants' tent; and, after being greeted with reproaches—uttered, however, in a very amiable tone of voice, and in Turkish—they venture to sit down by the fire, and our men make them a present of the head of a sheep, which they have just killed, in the Mussulman style, by severing the carotid arteries. They accept it with effusion when

Timour hands it to them, though they had turned their eyes away during the bloody sacrifice of a living creature. The observant Timour is astonished at their conduct, and remarks, "Just now, when Iça took his knife, they rushed upon him, and, holding his arm, begged him to let them kill the animal by strangling it with a cord round its nose. How could men eat a beast that has not been bled to death? When Iça killed it, they set to praying, and now they will gladly eat it. What strange people they are!"

The two men, being very hungry after their walk, hastily prepare their meal. They put a little water on the fire in some small earthenware pots, and when it is tepid, fill a wooden cup. They then take some meal out of long bags, sprinkle it with water, stir it round with their thumbs, and drink it; licking up the meal which sticks to the sides of the cup with their enormous tongues, which serve alike to show respect and admiration, and as spoons. Whilst they are drinking this "soup" to allay the pangs of hunger, the water begins to boil. They now pour it into their cups, put in some butter, likewise taken from a bag, and add a pinch of salt and a handful of meal. This mixture they then make into balls, which they go on eating until they have had enough; afterwards they take a little walk. When they return they proceed to occupy themselves with the sheep's head. From a leathern sheath each draws a small knife with pointed blade, such as even the women all wear at their waists, and cut the already frozen head to pieces. Then they draw near the fire and thaw it, burning off the wool in the flames. The skin being removed, they cut out and eat the gums; then, in order to get at the tongue, they draw a long sabre, with which they split the jaw open at the joints, removing both the tongue and the gullet, which they put in their wallets. One takes the lower jaw, and gets what he can off it, just like a dog would, while the other cleans the skull. The first gouges out the eyes, which he swallows with great relish; then when they have got off everything in the way of meat, and have satisfied their hunger, they throw the lower part of the head to the dogs, who certainly will not get much off it, and put aside for to-morrow the skull, which still contains the brains. The culinary art is decidedly in

THIBETAN SAVAGES ROUND A FIRE.

its infancy in Thibet, and we shall still, for a long time, be the only persons who have ever partaken of cabbage-soup there. Moreover, even the highest personages do not seem to have developed a delicate palate; the Amban himself, when in a hurry, eating balls of *zamba*. This afternoon, too, we happened to see at dinner the two interpreters—one of whom is, it seems, a lama endowed with a rich "stall." They had been served with a cup containing, at the bottom, a morsel of rancid butter and some meal. These they kneaded together, then adding some slices of frozen cheese, which was also worked in, they next minced into it a slice of frozen mutton, and then, to complete the dainty dish, they moistened it with tea and butter, finally making the whole mixture into balls, some of which they offered to us, as they saw that we were watching their preparations with great curiosity.

This powdered mixture is, with the addition of a little salt, eatable, and must be satisfying; while the making of it is an amusing pastime when one has nothing else to do, as was evidently the case with our lamas.

March 19.—We advance as far as Soubrou, to reach which we have to make numerous detours. The weather is abominable, for it is snowing, and the wind is blowing from the west with extreme violence. Here we find some twenty tents in a grassy valley, which is reached by a steep pass.

March 21.—After crossing a tableland we reach Di-Ti, where we drop down into an amphitheatre, formed by gently undulating hills. In the direction of Lhassa there are some heights white with snow, but we see very little to the east and north.

Di-Ti is on the main road from Naptchou to Lhassa, that of the Tsaïdam and of the Koukou Nor rising southward. We remain three days at Di-Ti, which is inhabited by a considerable number of nomads, who own large flocks of yaks and sheep that are swarming in every direction. They seem also to occupy themselves with the breeding of horses, some forty of which come to drink in the spring near our tent. They are larger than any we have come across so far, and have good legs and feet. No one is looking after them. Some distance away from our little fountain there is another, to which the people of the encampment go to draw their water, which they carry away in wooden jars. Attached to their loins they have a small cushion, and on this they place the jar with loose straps, which pass over their shoulders. The difficulty is to keep the jar so well balanced that no water is spilt on the way. To do this they walk with a forward stoop, the body forming nearly a right angle with the legs. A Thibetan couple came in quest of water while I was there. The wife filled the jar by means of a wooden cup, whilst the husband chatted with an acquaintance; she then helped him to fix the jar, which done, he went off, leaving his "better half" to get hers up as best she could. This she did by kneeling down and then carefully rising, like a beast of burden, as she really was.

March 24.—The maximum temperature in the sun reaches 89°. But the west wind still troubles us at times, though, it is true, it also provides us with something to talk about, as it drives before it on the plain clouds of dust, which assume very singular shapes. At one time you might fancy that an immense dragon with bent back was advancing, at another that a scorpion was crawling along with head and tongue raised, or again you might think you were looking at rows of trees with bushy foliage and leafy arches. All this time, however, we never forget the object we have in view, which is to reach Batang; and at last, after a warlike display, we extract a promise that we shall be directed thither. But the stages must be short, for the couriers from Llassa have not yet arrived; and so the Ta-Lama and the Ta-Amban, who have decided not to keep us waiting here any longer, send a special courier to Lhassa to hasten the despatch of the various articles we require, and of the other horses and presents from the authorities. Then we start. Every risk of a misunderstanding has now disappeared. Thibetans and Frenchmen are in thorough accord, and they, as well as we, are of opinion that the authorities at Lhassa are abusing our patience, and that bureaucracy has its disadvantages, though it may sometimes have its advantages.

Before I proceed with the account of our journey I would say a word or two about the inhabitants of this country, who are well-to-do and prosperous, especially when compared with the first shepherds whom we met. More favourable conditions have the same effect on the men as on the yaks and horses; all of them are more vigorous here, and they are even slightly taller. The types, as I have said before, are very varied. Some have a long nose and a broad face, others a snub nose and a long face; others, again, a long nose and a long face. They have, however, some points in common. Their chins are often prominent because they are frequently toothless, and their lips are very thick because the cold makes them swell, and because they continually use them, their shortness of breath making them wheeze. Again, when they stop they stand erect, very straight on their legs, which are a little apart; their gait is jerky, their glance shifting and rapid, though sometimes fixed; their gestures are abrupt; and they walk with short irregular steps, as though their thoughts were intermittent, and their brains suggested actions by fits and starts in intervals of wakefulness. In fact, all their gestures suggest a lack of mental cohesion and a poverty of ideas.

They are careless and cheerful in disposition, and after a long day's march they go to look for the yaks, singing and laughing, some bringing in the droppings for fuel, while others carry sheets of ice in the skirts of their cloaks. They tie up their yaks in a half-circle, chattering all the time; at night prepare the cords for the morning, and, having eaten their *zamba*, put their wallets round the fire; and then, loosening the girdle of their cloaks, throw themselves down on the ground side by side, the one who is most exposed to the wind protecting himself with a coarse mantle. Lying there, huddled together like sheep, they exchange a few words, and then fall asleep under the stars, with the temperature below zero.

March 27.—As we advance we find the country more thickly populated, and it seems as though the desert is coming to an end.

March 28.—This is a day never to be forgotten. The road we are following is that of Sininfou; it is dotted with numerous trees, under which are massed together numberless prayers engraved on slabs of schist, with attempts at ornamentation—roses, for example, each petal of which contains a syllable of the

"Om mané padmé houm," images of Buddha, of Tsong Kaba the reformer, and of the Talai-Lama, sketched in outline on plates, or moulded in clay—each of these holy personages having his head enveloped in a hood and surrounded with a halo. The road winds across the broad plains, interspersed with valleys and ravines, and topped towards the south-west by white ridges which intercept the horizon. We are at a height of barely 16,000 feet, and it is less painful to breathe. The wind has fallen, and before us slowly gather large white clouds, above which the sky is a spotless blue, while below larks are singing, and small rats are running about on the ground.

It is hot, really hot, and the warm breeze, as it caresses our cheeks, produces quite a novel sensation, for we had lost all recollection of so pleasant a feeling. We advance in the best of spirits, urged on by our horses, which keep their noses in our backs. Then we mount them, and for the first time since last autumn our feet are really warm in the stirrup, even "on the shady side," although it does not thaw there as yet.

The Amban, followed by his escort, joins us and salutes us —with a very good pronunciation—in the few French words that we have taught him.

"Bonjour," he says; "comment vous portez-vous?"

"Very well," we answer.

"Bien, bien," he repeats with a smile.

He raises his whip, and his horse starts off at a trot, for he is anxious to arrive first, so as to prepare the encampment.

But here is a Thibetan horseman, who arrives at a gallop, with his rifle slung over his shoulders, and a little red flag floating from the sight. From his girdle hangs a sabre with glittering incrustations; his right arm is freed from his cloak, and his shoulder is bare, and he excites his horse by swinging his sling. He is a good specimen of a wild horseman, and the picture is heightened by his fox-skin cap, with long ear-flaps hanging

THE TA-LAMA, THE TA-AMBAN, AND OTHER CHIEFS FROM LHASSA.

down, from under which appear a few loose hairs and a long plait, which continually strikes against his shoulders.

Next comes a lama, wearing a hood and closely wrapped up, accompanying some yaks that are loaded with precious objects. He joins our party, reciting his prayers aloud, and salutes us with an amiable smile, though without interrupting a single word of his litany. Then we pass three men on foot who are urging on their yaks, whistling and waving their right arms about. The body of one is quite bare, and displays a rounded chest; he is stout and broad-shouldered. With his muscular right arm he balances a long javelin with a bamboo handle, attached to his wrist by a copper bracelet. To show his skill he throws it in the air and catches it again, then shifts it from one hand to the other and round his body, brandishing it as though about to strike, with all the grace of a skilled matador. He is young, and walks with a supple swing; his jaws and square chin are prominent, and his upper lip is arched with the insolent curl of an animal that knows its own strength. His nose is short, with broad nostrils; his bushy hair hangs down, like a mane, covering his small eyes and foreshortening his face, causing his head, with its thick neck, to look still broader and less human. You would think you had before you a specimen of early man just emerging from the Stone Age, and proud in the possession of his first iron weapon.

But it is time to return to the Amban's tent to partake of tea and butter, boiled mutton, smoked tongues, and even Indian curry—for they quite spoil us. Everyone is most polite—so much so, in fact, that we no longer dare even look at them, for fear of seeing those monstrous tongues hanging out.

We have reached Nigan, at a height of 15,900 feet, and it is here that we shall have to wait for the last time before setting out for Batang, whence we shall be conveyed by the aid of the Talai-Lama; for the oracles have been favourable to us.

We employ this last stoppage in doing up our baggage again,

looking over and arranging the skins which we have dressed on the road. We get rid of everything that is not absolutely necessary, and organise the caravan of those who will leave us to return to the Lob Nor. The Ta-Lama undertakes to put them in charge of some pilgrims who are returning to Mongolia by the Tsaïdam, and once there they will continue their journey alone by the Kalmucks' road. We now feel quite close to Tonquin, for, though thousands of miles lie between it and us, at Batang we shall again tread known ground. Then doubt, which is the defect—or perhaps it should rather be said, the good point—of old travellers, reappears. The horizon darkens, and in the far distance obstacles arise. However, things are turning out remarkably well.

March 31.—After a calm night and a minimum of 4° below zero, a hurricane bursts over us, and a fearful squall carries off the square tents of the Thibetans. Ours resist the force of the storm, and are merely invaded by clouds of dust.

April 2.—At last the Amban comes beaming to tell us that the Talai-Lama's presents have arrived, as well as all the things which we asked for, and to invite us to come to his tent, where the Ta-Lama and the Ta-Amban await us. We are very well received by these great chiefs, and have a long talk with them. Then the presents are spread out before us—costumes of women, men, lamas, and other great personages; every imaginable kind of head-gear, objects of veneration, skins, prayer-mills, scented wood, and even packets of prayers. They explain to us the use of each object, and tell us its name, its material, and its origin. On examining the costumes we are surprised to find many European fashions among them—crinolines, pinafores, earrings, a coiffure shaped like a diadem, and every form of bonnet, including caps with flaps for the ears, hoods, and a minister's (*kaloun*) hat, which is astonishingly like that of a cardinal, with its cords and tassels. Among the sacred objects are bells, rosaries, and lights, to remind us of the Catholic ritual. Our first idea is that these objects are relics of a time when the Thibetans doubtless professed the same faith as we do, and though they have now

A THIBETAN SALUTING.

long lost it, they have retained some of its externals. But with regard to these questions I must refer my readers to the admirable narrative of Father Huc, and to the works of our missionaries in Thibet, Biet, Desgodins, etc., who have been able to study them still more closely than Father Huc, and with an ability to which I cannot pretend. During the interview they cram us with dainties; aromatics are burning all the time, and often a servant enters with perfume, which he sprinkles over the hot coals; the first cloud is addressed to Buddha, the second is offered to us, and passed under, and even up, our noses. They treat us as though we were gods. But the certainty that we are at last really going towards Batang contributes even more than these attentions to put us one and all in good-humour. The Amban manifests his great pleasure at things having come to so gratifying a conclusion, for, in his character of intermediary between his chiefs and us, he has been exposed to rebuffs and maledictions, and to the reproaches of his chiefs when he had to tell them that he had failed in his mission.

The horses destined for us arrived this evening, and excellent ones they are too, but not shod, and our endeavours to fix shoes on them are all in vain, for their hoofs are so hard, dry, and friable that the nails bend or fail to hold, or actually split them.

April 4.—We have offered our presents in return to the Thibetans, regarding it as a point of honour to surpass them in generosity, so that we almost emptied our packets in making them happy. Revolvers, watches, mirrors, as well as knives and scissors, were in great request, while gold coin and silver roubles were highly appreciated. Small silver coins, too, are accepted with pleasure, for they will serve as buttons in the Chinese fashion. As it is, two or three lamas of high rank have buttons made of quarter-rupees.

They all seemed to be very much pleased with our offerings, but whether or not we actually succeeded in satisfying the wants of the forty or fifty chiefs and servants with whom we had had to do, I cannot say. At all events, when we parted, our farewell had every appearance of cordiality, and they left nothing undone to facilitate our journey as far as Batang, supplying us with provisions, such as rice, meal, barley, beans, and small peas, and giving us advice as to what we should be able to purchase on the road, and what we must save up.

They gave us a lama to act as our guide, and introduce us to the chiefs of the numberless tribes we shall encounter. He is a great, strong fellow of about twenty-five, looks very good-natured, and later on proved himself a man with a good head, very cool, and very astute. His superiors urge him to serve us faithfully, and obey us promptly, and to ensure his doing so, make him presents before we start, and promise him still more valuable ones if he brings back proofs of our satisfaction. This young lama, who has already been this journey once, will be accompanied by a long-haired chief, whose business it is to maintain order amongst the score of savages who are to transport our baggage and supplies by means of some sixty yaks. In a fortnight this chief will make way for another, to whom he will hand over the Ta-Lama's orders, and so on, as long as we are on ground that is subject to them, while the lamas of independent tribes will help us at the request of our lama guide.

The Ta-Amban, who has been to Batang, and knows the tribes that we shall meet, gave us some very fatherly advice with regard to them. "You will, on the road, meet with some wild tribes, whose ways are very rough, for they are totally uncivilised; but only have patience with them, and all will be well. The worst you will find near Batang, and when you reach that district be on your guard, for a European was once killed there, and a Chinese mandarin stoned. Do not, therefore, neglect measures of precaution. As for us, we shall pray for you, and we can only hope that you will have a prosperous journey."

The Ta-Lama approved of this advice, and promised us his prayers, which he thinks will be efficacious. We then shook hands with them both, and mounted our horses; and amid the farewell salutations of the whole body, chiefs and all, a start was made.

THE LAMA GUIDE.

A few miles farther on we encamped for the night, and the Amban caught us up to assure himself of the perfect organisation of our caravan, and to watch over the safe return to their own country of those of our servants who are leaving us.

Great are the rejoicings of our whole band, including the three dogs who gambol around us. Even our ram bounds with

AN ATTENDANT OF THE AMBAN.

delight—for we have with us, as a companion of our travels, a big ram from Kourla. He is quite tame, and we have not sacrificed him to our hunger. Now he is everybody's friend, is permitted to sleep in a tent, takes bread from our hands, and even scents it out and abstracts it from our bags for himself. He is very courageous, too, charging dogs and horses, and when we purchase other sheep, butts them out of jealousy. At the beginning of our travels, before we got into the Lob Nor district, he used to mix with the others and lead them, but now he will neither follow his fellows nor walk with the baggage. Nothing less than the society of his masters will satisfy him, and he runs bleating behind us as though to complain that we are going too fast. Macha, for that is his name, has often cheered our drooping spirits, and still more often aroused the astonishment of the Thibetans by his size, and especially by his enormously fat tail.

April 5.—The return of Timour, Parpa, Iça, and the three Dungans was settled yesterday, and they have received all that they require, provisions, horses, money, and some presents. But our three Mussulmans asked permission to spend the night with their comrades, and to help them in starting for the east to-day. They assist them in packing the tent, superintend the loading, and exchange a few small objects which will remind them of each other.

Whilst they are loading our yaks, we go to the Amban's tent to eat at his table for the last time. He gives a glass of spirits to all who ask for it, not knowing that men should never drink when travelling; and when the meal is over, there is soon a slight uproar which prevents the Amban and me from conversing. And Abdullah, our interpreter, does not miss this chance of getting intoxicated, so he cannot translate our remarks. The meeting is, therefore, brought to a close, and the Amban and his men accompany us on foot to our camp, where we find our three servants and Rachmed. The last yak is now loaded, part of our heavy baggage is already far ahead, and we must part. We commend once more, and for the last time, our three servants to the Amban's care, and then cordially shake hands with these honest fellows, whom we shall doubtless never see again. When we wish them good health and a safe return home, and beg them not to forget us, they burst into tears, fall on their knees, and kiss our hands, sobbing bitterly.

They then press Rachmed, Abdullah, and Akoun to their breasts, and those who are bound for the coast weep as well as those who are returning home. All these men have been connected with us in circumstances amid which men cannot conceal their real character, or be independent of their neighbours. They have suffered together, have had to help each other, and have learnt to esteem and really like each other. And now their hearts are very sad at parting. Their evident affection for us cannot but touch us, for it is spontaneous, and proceeds from men of energy, from adventurers perhaps, who are capable of doing one a bad turn, but whom we have made better men. They, too, are convinced that we like them, for we have taken as much care of them as of ourselves, and have never exacted from them an effort which was not needful, or reproached them without cause.

Again we shake hands with the Amban and his companions, who have been greatly moved by this scene, and he promises us that he will pray for us. And so we set out, accompanied for several yards by Parpa and his companions, who hold our horses' bridles as a mark of their respect.

We must, however, separate, and they raise their hands to their beards with a "Great is Allah!" and we there leave them desolate and in tears.

THIBETAN HORSEMAN.

CHAPTER XII.

SO AND ITS LAMA-HOUSE.

At Gatine—The River Ourtchou—A Hermit Lama—" Steeped in Luxury "—At Djaocounnene—Meeting a Caravan—Resemblance Between Thibetans and Other Peoples—Thumb Language—A Droll Native—The Thibetans Not Fanatics—On the Banks of the Omtchou—At Tandi—The Thibetan Sling—A Superb Mountain Scene—A Sight of Ploughed Land—First View of the Lama-house of So—The " Delicious Odour " of Wood—A *Concierge* in Thibet—Native Money—A Commission of 150 per cent.—Ploughing at So—Crossing the So-tchou—A Bearded Thibetan—Why Dishonest Chiefs are Popular.

MONUMENT NEAR THE LAMA-HOUSE OF SO.

OUR first stage to Batang lies through a valley that varies in breadth from one to four miles, with encampments in the gorges, and herds on the ridges. The Ourtchou, which flows down it, is, it seems, one of the three great tributaries of the Naptchou, which has several smaller ones as well. After four hours on horseback we encamp on a slight elevation, at a place called, as our guide tells us, Gatine.

Our tent is pitched on the edge of a rapid stream, from which all the ice and snow have disappeared, except in its creeks. We have descended some hundred yards while following first the bottom of the valley, and then the low hills that skirt it on the right. On the eastern slopes, a little vegetation is visible, consisting of brushwood half a foot high which bears in Central Asia the generic name of " Camel's Tail," and this suffices to " furnish " the landscape a little. The path is at times very stony, and at the lower end of the valley grows that stalky, strong grass, which is the despair of thinly shod people. Our direction is at present north-east, soon to change to east; in order to strike a road which, though far from being the straighter of the two, is, we are assured, the better for beasts of burden. We must needs follow our guide, for the simple reason that we cannot argue with him, from want of information, books having taught us nothing about this district, which is blank on the map. However, we think we recognise on the Russian maps the spot which we ought to reach in ten days, if our yak-drivers are right. Its name is So (written Sok), and we shall find there, we are told, a large lama-house. Our stay at Gatine is most enjoyable; at three p.m. the thermometer marks 41° in the shade. Taking my gun, I go for a walk on the tableland, and feel a real pleasure in being quite alone, without any of the Thibetans with whom we have to talk and argue for hours together.

The shadows gradually darken on the mountain-side, which does not look steep. It seems, by insensible degrees, to form stages up to the very top, so as not to put the climber out of breath. Northwards the horizon is still bathed in light, while over the valley float trails of bluish smoke betraying the presence of tents. The quiet is delicious, broken only by the larks, lustily trilling their love-songs. Presently night begins to fall. The sun is lost to sight, after seeming to rest a moment on the bend of the tableland to the west. No sooner, however, has he run his daily course, than the moon rises in the east, like an immense ball of gold, in the direction of Batang. Then, suddenly, two wolves appear on the top of a snow-hill, but, seeing me, stop, and after a moment's reflection, turn tail. As they were out of range at first, and are now far away, it is useless to think of following them, so I return to the camp to warn our men that they must protect our flock of sheep. They accordingly tie the older ones together, nose to nose, by their horns, and the others, of their own accord, creep in between them. Over sixty yaks are also attached, in a ring, to a cord fixed close to the ground, so as to form, with their hairy bodies, a wall round our tents and sheep, a small gap being left in the circle so that we may have an open path to draw water from the stream. The horses are left to wander at will around the camp, as we know that they are accustomed and able to protect themselves against the wolves, and in case of danger our dogs will give the alarm.

Our drivers having asked us to start early the following morning, so that the yaks may have time to graze during the day, we soon get supper ready, consisting of boiled mutton, which we attack with a good appetite. Above us shine the stars, though very feebly in the dazzling moonshine; a gentle breeze comes from the south, not a single cloud is to be seen, and the heavens display all their grandeur, the mountains being apparently reduced, under so magnificent a vault, to the size of mere molehills.

The road is no longer dull as it was in winter: the landscape is more varied, game is abundant and furnishes plenty of distraction. Our collection becomes by degrees our chief care, for the nomads we come across are as affable as possible. They live in black tents, drinking the milk of their cows, which are very small, and which they cross with yaks. They have sheep with very fine wool, and also small goats about the size of our kids. The goats are generally black, with long drooping hair like the yaks, small horns, and legs that look short but are undoubtedly strong, as is proved by their bounds and speed; they weigh from eleven to thirteen pounds. The wives of the Thibetan shepherds have to do nearly all the work, but they enjoy full liberty, and are not unsociable, freely approaching our camp, sitting down by the side of our Thibetans, and soon getting to be on good terms with them.

April 6.—We have been lost in admiration of the dwelling of a hermit lama perched on the mountain, on the left bank of the river Ourtchou, between Gatine and Tsatang, for it is so long since we have seen anything like a house. This looked a very large one, but our lama told us that it was very small—just large enough for one person. With the help of our glasses we could make out a rectangle of chalk walls, a verandah, and the frames of one window and one door, so that it must really be quite small. But it was bathed in sunshine, and looked so white and cheerful that we could not pity the monk who has retired there, away from the distractions of the world. We asked our lama how this recluse could live, and he pointed to the tents that are pitched lower down in the valley: "They give him all he needs: whenever he wants anything, he goes down to those tents and prays, then they fill his wallet, and he returns home."

Considerable difficulty is experienced in getting our yaks to cross the river. For the breaking-up of the frost is now near at hand, and the edges are already clear of ice; and we have to enter the water, then mount on ice, repeating this performance several times before gaining the opposite bank. The laden yaks break through and fall into the water, only extricating themselves with great difficulty, and after wetting our baggage, though it is protected by felt wrappings.

The width of the river varies from 160 to 350 feet, and in flood may be 470 feet near Tsatang, where it widens out. Then it penetrates the mountain, which contracts it, and causes it to wind gently. Near Gatine it broadens out again and forms cyots on which we see and kill some ruddy sheldrakes (*Casarca rutila*); the same, I think, that are found in Turkestan, and called in Turkish, if I remember aright, *dourma*. Along this same river, too, we kill some geese with heads striped with black, ducks exactly like those of the Lob Nor, white gulls, and a crane, such as Prjevalsky first described.

All our wants are supplied at the encampments which we come across: very good mutton, plenty of milk, fuel, water in skins when we are no longer on the banks of the river, and fodder for our beasts. We are short of nothing, so well does our lama, seconded by a young chief who has a long plait of hair, look after us; in fact, they take as much care of us as if they were our sons. Compared to the life we were leading only a short time ago, and especially before we reached Dam, we feel ourselves positively steeped in luxury.

Now and again we meet with hunters carrying matchlocks, forks, and lances, with powerful dogs in leash, long-haired, like our shepherds' dogs, and with broad heads shaped like that of a bear. Many of these dogs are black, with reddish-brown spots, this latter being generally the colour of their chests and paws, as it is that of the hares to the south of the higher tablelands. We collect quantities of small birds, and come across black divers, black marmots, and dark brown bears.

In proportion as we advance the natives improve in face and form, and we are much struck by their gaiety and light-heartedness. The women smear their faces with butter, and, as they never wash, the butter catches the smoke and dust and becomes a regular mask of soot. We can only suppose that they do this in order to protect their faces against the biting winds.

April 8.—At Djaucounnene, after turning in an easterly direction on quitting a pass, we for the first time meet a caravan. Bags are piled up to form a wall behind which the travellers take shelter, whilst their yaks graze close by. They are transporting barley and meal from So to Lhassa. As they approach we are struck by the breadth of their faces, and the slant of their eyes, which turn upwards at the corners; they are dressed just like our drivers, but are much taller.

At first sight, a new people presents a well-defined general type; but, on looking more closely, and examining it well, this apparent uniformity is found to be qualified by considerable variety. We are even astonished to find a resemblance in our Thibetans to certain other nations, and even to friends and acquaintances of ours. Here, for instance, is one with a perfect Greek profile, as shown on the best cameos. His neighbour, on the other hand, is of the redskin type, with receding brow and arched nose, like

THIBETAN OF THE REDSKIN TYPE.

an eagle's beak, while he walks with head slightly thrown back. By his side is a young lad, singing as he prepares some meat for sausages, cutting it on the pommel of his saddle; with his dark eyes and regular features, and hair falling over his forehead, he might be an Italian. What we can affirm as a fact is that we are in the presence of a white race, that has nothing in common with those of a yellow complexion but the absence of beard, which is, however, amply compensated by the quantity of hair they have on their heads; in fact, it is not unusual to see even old men with plaits as thick as a cable.

Our yak-drivers are always busy, content with little sleep, and very cheerful; all the time they are getting their beasts ready they hum an air, and finish the loading very quickly. They are indefatigable walkers, and some of them climb the steepest hillsides singing and without losing breath; in fact, they breathe with greater ease than do their yaks, though we should bear in mind that these latter are loaded. Deep-chested, these men have well-set necks, of average length. To-day Rachmed made them a present of half a sheep, as a proof of our being well satisfied with them. Using their knives with the greatest dexterity, they put the best pieces aside, ate the head raw, as we had seen them do before, and proceeded to cook the rest by throwing the inferior pieces into hot water, the feet with the wool still on them, and the intestines scarcely cleansed.

They are excellent mimics, and speak very well, with a good deal of gesture and facial play. I have already explained that they express disagreement by joining the thumb-nails, and agreement by putting them just the opposite way. Putting the thumb up means approval and satisfaction; raising the little finger denotes hostility, while to keep it in this position and at the same time to shake the head signifies dislike. The two thumbs placed perpendicularly one above the other, with the tongue hanging out, denote superlative approval.

The old man who was photographed, prayer-mill in hand, is very droll, and fond of jokes. Our interpreter Abdullah amuses himself by saluting him in Thibetan. When the old man replies, with astounding seriousness, Abdullah asks him how he salutes a chief like the Amban, and the old man lolls out his tongue and bows low; and when anyone speaks to him of the Ta-Amban (Great Amban), he expresses the deepest degree of humility by scratching himself behind the ear. We laugh, and the Thibetans themselves are amused by this little comedy.

It often happens that our lama prays aloud, as well as the young chief, his companion. Then Abdullah begins to imitate their different intonations of voice, so that we cannot tell which is which; far from being angry, they all, "clerics" as well as laymen, begin to laugh. This does not suggest religious fanaticism; they seem, indeed, to content themselves with the forms and externals of religion, as the sole manifestation of their faith. Our old chief occupies his leisure moments in turning his prayer-mill from right to left, even when walking, and often mumbles a litany. Men who believe in the transmigration of souls, and to whom intellectual exercise is a thing unknown, can only occupy themselves usefully, when neither legs nor arms are working, in reciting formulas under the impression that they will thus secure for themselves a better existence.

April 9.—The day before yesterday we left the river Ourtchou to ascend one of its tributaries, called the Botchou; on the 8th we traversed a tableland and a pass into a valley where the Ourtchou flows in a south-easterly direction. We therefore had to leave it again, and to-day we ascended a small river towards the east, encamping at the upper end of a valley, at the foot of a pass which we shall ascend to-morrow. We are, at present, at an altitude of from 15,000 to 16,000 feet. In the valleys, where grass is to be found, we saw some tents and flocks. Three men whom we met were as much alike as three brothers could be. They were all short, and had the round heads, and straight noses, with narrow bridges, of Romans. All three were toothless, and, with their lower lips drooping on to their round chins, they recalled the busts of Nero.

We are now on the banks of the Omtchou, but shall have to leave it, for it, too, flows south-east, as far as we can tell, as is the case with most of the rivers in this region.

April 10.—A pass leads us to a small river, then another limestone pass, with *obos*, on which our Thibetans do not fail to deposit stones with a prayer; then another valley, and a river to cross, and finally a steppe from three to four miles broad, which seems a vast plain. Through it flows the So-tchou, which is from 100 to 200 feet broad. According to what our lama and the old chief say, we have now crossed the four

YAK-DRIVER WITH PRAYER-MILL (p. 78).

principal tributaries of the Kitchou, which flows by Lhassa, viz., the Ourtchou, the Poptchou, the Omdjamtchou, and the Satchou.

April 12.—We have a sharp white frost during the night, but the morning is superb. Antelopes stare at us, great eagles are describing circles in the air, and in the gorge our hunters see some bears. These animals swarm about here, and, unfortunately for us, have better legs than their pursuers. Wolves often howl at night, but are never visible by day. We traverse a pass, at a height of about 16,500 feet, and encamp, at the bottom, at Tandi, on the banks of a river.

Our stages, it will be seen, are very similar to one another. We do not feel them to be severe, for we are now much better and stronger, but they average twelve miles each, which means a good deal more in a mountainous country than elsewhere. In order that our yaks may not lose strength, their loads are changed every day, so that the same beast never carries our wild-yak skins, which are very heavy, nor our cartridge-boxes, on two successive days. As soon as one is tired, it is unloaded, and another takes its place out of a reserve stock of ten, which only carry their saddles.

April 13.—We begin to ascend from the moment of starting, and for three hours follow the deviations of a path which winds along the side of the ridges, now to the south-east, now to the north-east. To the north are steep heights and bare rocks, while to the south valleys descend towards a smaller chain, also bare, beyond and overlooking which is a higher chain, white with ice glittering from under the snow. The road is difficult, and we admire the agility of our yaks, their surefootedness, and the strength of their legs, thanks to which they can take a drop of six feet and fall on their feet, and that, too, with a load on their backs. And our horses are quite as clever.

A caravan meets us on its way to Lhassa, consisting, of course, of *no* (as yaks are called in these parts), for everything here is transported by these cattle with horses' tails. They are laden with long boxes covered with skins, and containing sugar, as we are told. At the head marches a lama with a pointed yellow cap, and carrying over his shoulder his cup in a leather bag, and several sacred images in little frames of hammered copper. He walks quickly, and his leanness, his hollow cheeks, and light step, remind Rachmed and me of old Pir, a good mollah who was our guide on the Pamir. The descent is along a river with high banks, and intercepted with ravines. Then the valley contracts to a mere gorge between the rocks, which we descend on ice, and the gorge in turn becomes a valley. We camp at Tjéma-Loung, which means "mouth of the gorge." Some tents are pitched not far off, and when we pass in front of them, the dogs rush out at us, but their masters call them back and drive them away with stones, and then salute us. They have come here to prostrate themselves before their chief (*bembo*), whose face is pitted with small-pox. He is, however, very energetic, and accompanies us as long as we are on the grounds of his tribe. His insignia consist of a collar and bells, which he hangs round his horses' neck. We repeatedly ask for milk, and the chief never fails to demand some at the tents which we pass, though he coolly pockets all the small change which we hand to those who provide us with it.

Around our tents lammergeiers are fighting over the remains of a sheep, which they watched us kill. Wishing to see for ourselves the skill of the Thibetans with the sling, we asked a man to try his aim at one about seventy-five yards off. Picking out an oval stone, a young man, who passes for the best slinger amongst them, places it in the sling, then swings it round once; the end cracks, and the stone falls within nine inches of the bird, which flies off at once. We examine this redoubtable weapon, which is about seven feet in length and very simple, consisting of strands of wool plaited loosely together, so as to leave it supple. In the middle is a small pocket to hold the stone. At one end is a ring in which the thumb is placed, the other end, having no ring, is pressed between the thumb and the finger, care being taken that the stone hangs evenly in the middle.

To-night our men keep on the alert. Some of them sleep at a certain distance from the tents, watching the yaks. From time to time those near the tents give forth shrill cries, and the distant sentinels reply with a similar cry, which is again given back like an echo by the men on the mountains. It is a sort of greeting to each other, as well as a defiance to the enemy, for we are told that caravans are often robbed hereabouts.

April 14.—We set out early for So, which is on the other side of some difficult passes. After crossing the river and then one of its affluents, we mounted to the top of the first pass, which is about 13,000 feet high. Then, by a path which is stony, difficult, and such that a horse cannot always get up with his rider, in four hours we reached the Ia-La, at an altitude of about 16,500 feet. These excellent people here rightly thought that we should be glad of a draught of milk, which is as welcome as manna in this stony desert, where our only drink is snow that has been sheltered from the sun at the bottom of the crevasses.

After satisfying our hunger and thirst, we continue our journey by a path along a ridge as far as the *obo* that marks the spot where the desert commences. A perfect panorama here stretches out before our eyes. The horizon is clear at the four cardinal points, and a regular ocean of mountains is visible; quite as many to the north as to the south, only the summits are whiter southwards. This is undoubtedly a magnificent mountain scene, though these "grand views" are, after all, very much alike, and a little stretch of plain would be most acceptable.

After such a climb, it is only right that we should have a scramble down. At one time we go faster than we care for on a stony path with innumerable twists, at another we slide along rocks on the ice left by a torrent, falling and then getting up again. We do not lose a single one of our loaded yaks, but among those which are not laden, three fall over a precipice, and are killed at once. We then cross, recross, and again cross the river, to find ourselves on such level ground that our horses, of their

A LOADED YAK.

own accord, break into a trot. To our left, at the lower end of the plateau, is a river flowing from the north to the south, into which the one we have just crossed empties itself. But what is it that we see in the valley? Cultivated fields! Ploughed land!

Yes, and farther away to the north, at the junction of the rivers, a sort of pyramid, looking like a sugar-loaf on a cubic base of masonry. Insensibly the ground rises, and soon, straight in front of us, upon an isolated cone which the river skirts to the east, rise high grey walls, built on the very edge of the cliffs and forming a most imposing mass. Above these walls extends a rectangle, having at one end a square tower and at the other a cloistered gallery. From the flat roof rise long poles looking like masts, from the ends of which float coloured flags and pennants.

The chief who is our guide, tells us that this is So Goumba, the lama-house of So. As he pronounced these words, the poor savage's face expressed his pride, and he repeated "So Goumba! So Goumba!" as though he would give us to understand that it is not every day that one has the luck to see so fine an edifice. As for us, although we did not feel his admiration for this specimen of human work, yet the sight of a habitation was a real satisfaction to us. For five months we had not seen so extensive, so monumental a building; indeed, I might say for six, for the huts and cottages at Tcharkalik scarcely count.

Our curiosity was now aroused, for we had heard before from our men that there are many houses at So, and we were therefore naturally anxious to arrive there. But as we proceeded we saw nothing beyond what I have described. At last I asked, "Where is So?"

"There it is," answered the Thibetan, pointing with his finger to what we were unwilling to take for a town. We congratulated him on the beauty of his capital, and one man, taking our remarks quite seriously, expressed his acquiescence. On reaching the Goumba, we discovered that it looks like a fortress only on the north and west sides, and that the winds are the enemy against which these solid walls have been reared as a defence. The south front presents to view row upon row of small limestone houses, exposed to the sun's rays, which they admit by doors, windows, and countless galleries. This side is as open as the others are shut in. All the dwellings, clinging to the sides of the slopes and the irregularities in the rock, are so completely one above the other, that the roofs of one row serve as terrace or courtyard to those in the row above. The one wide opening is the gate, flanked by pillars in the Persian style, and by this the bearers of sacks, faggots, and other necessaries destined for the use of the monastery enter and depart.

The good lamas were to be seen with bare heads and shorn, draped, like Roman senators, in dark, coarse woollen robes; some walking up and down the terraces, others sitting cross-legged or stretched on rugs, with their legs tucked under them, and watching us as they basked in the sunshine.

Wending our way to the palace we were to occupy, we came to a gate with folding doors, to which are affixed two written notices in Thibetan, which, with the aid of the imagination, enabled us to fancy that they were lodging us in the Town Hall of the district. Through a porch we entered a square court, in the north-west corner of which some small chambers are built against the walls, with a gallery, constructed of wooden pillars, in front of them. The other two sides of the court contain only a granary, and a place where the horses are tethered.

This house is, it seems, reserved for the reception of great men on their way to or from Lhassa, and belongs to the Talai-Lama, that is, the oligarchy which rules Thibet. A pole—dressed at the top with stuffs of every colour, yellow predominating—rising from the courtyard, marks the fact that it is under the Government flag. A simple glance at the interior of these so-called "rooms" sufficed to make us decide to keep to our tents, so full were they of filth and vermin.

While our men were erecting our tent, after levelling the ground a little, we made for a heap of split wood against the wall.

Wood! imagine our happiness as we feel it, and sniff the delicious odour of the still green juniper, which penetrates even to our hearts, Frenchmen as we are, who love the forests so keenly, and whose ancestors used to cry, "To the mistletoe!" on New Year's Day. Then we were lost in ecstasy before their walls, built, as is the fashion out here, with rough stones and soil, and sanctified by the insertion of prayers and carved images of Buddha. Our attention was next attracted by the roof, with its astonishing, unheard-of chimney-top, consisting of a huge earthenware pot that had lost its bottom, probably by being knocked against an iron one; by garlands of prayers, attached to staples and decorating our house; by the stairs, made of earth and turf, leading up to the roof; and by the fireside, a little square altar, on which were odoriferous branches in honour of the divinity. Finally, to complete the house, was a *concierge*, living in a little lodge, with a bitch and her two puppies. He was an ugly-looking individual, greasy, tall, lean, and squint-eyed, with a pointed face black with filth, and made apparently longer by his high narrow forehead; he had the short hair of a lama, and seemed to be a sort of lay-brother. We were scarcely settled when we received a visit from the civil and the religious chiefs, who were both very polite to us, bringing us rice, milk, two sheep, and chopped straw for our horses. They made a note of what we wanted, and gave us their word that we should be able to start in two days without fail, in accordance with our wishes. We made them some presents in turn. In the evening they cooked us some excellent slices of mutton, thanks to a good wood fire, and we had capital milk, well-made bread and well-cooked rice. We could sit near the fire without being poisoned by the smell of the dried dung which they burn in the desert; and, in truth, we fancied ourselves in another world. We were now at a height of less than 10,000 feet, and the air seemed so heavy and so stifling that we had to open the door of our tent. At nightfall the lamas, posted on the terraces of the monastery, gave us a serenade with their long trumpets, the dogs supplementing this discordant music with their barking; but the awful noise gradually diminished, and so we fell asleep.

April 15.—When we awoke this morning we complained of the heat. The minimum during the night was only 23° Fahr., so that winter is over for us, and not too soon. Having spent the day mending various articles, we distributed presents among the senior chiefs and drivers who have accompanied us, as they wished to start on their way back before sunset, so that they might spend the night at the foot of Ia-La, and commence its difficult ascent to-morrow.

We paid them generously in *iambas*, though they prefer Indian rupees to this species of money in bulk; because the Chinese merchants constantly cheat them by having two different scales, which always tell in their own favour, and also by preparing a very bad alloy; not unnaturally, therefore, the savages prefer actual coins, the weight and value of which they understand. The only Thibetan coin that we have seen used is one about as thick as a sixpence and as large as a halfpenny, weighing the sixth of an ounce. It ought always to be of silver, but sometimes, to the disgrace of the authorities of the "mint," it is of a bad alloy, so that the savages do not readily accept it. On one side it is stamped with inscriptions on eight medallions, forming a circle round a rose in the centre; and on the other, with curious ornamentations, among which we fancy we can recognise the crescent touching the sun, and the trident.

This distribution of money and presents gave rise to a little incident, and revealed to us the presence of a Chinaman at So, a confirmed opium-smoker, who gains a livelihood as a usurer and money-changer. He is a native of Kensi, and was obliged, long ago, to flee his country for good and sufficient reasons. We availed ourselves of his knowledge of Thibetan to explain to

THE LAMA-HOUSE AT SO.

the men whom we had been rewarding the amount of the money which we had given them; for, with the exception of the oldest amongst them, they had no idea of the meaning of scales and weights. And the chiefs who accompanied us, having offered to exchange these ingots for "cash," had given them only three or four apiece of these Thibetan coins, thus realising a profit of one hundred and fifty per cent. When the opium-smoker explained our generosity to them, they were very much put out at the rapacity of their chiefs, though the majority of them dared neither protest nor ask for their ingots back. Two, however, did not conceal their displeasure, and we intervened and made the chiefs hand back to the poor fellows what was meant for them, whereupon they manifested their joy by jumping about in most comical fashion. Then, bowing down and taking our hands, they placed them on their heads, and finally withdrew backwards, raising their thumbs and hanging out their tongues. Their yaks were quickly assembled and loaded with their slender baggage, and they started off singing.

The news of our arrival having got abroad, with the addition, no doubt, that we were open-handed, our house was positively besieged by a crowd of beggars of both sexes. We offered them a sheep, which we handed to the captain of this horde, bidding him distribute it equally. This largess rid us of them and their vermin, but not of the dogs. The number of these animals is perfectly astounding; in fact, we could not say whether beggars or dogs were the more numerous at So.

From our house we can see the men ploughing in the valley below. They scratch the mountain-side with a plough drawn by two yaks, which are led by a man who holds the cords attached to the rings in their noses. From behind the ploughman whips them up, though they do not go any quicker, but merely straighten their tufted tails and growl. The furrows are very small, and as far as possible perpendicular to the lie of the slope, with the view, no doubt, of stopping the waters which run down from the plateau. When the field has been ploughed they come towards us, and so give us the opportunity of examining their team. It consists of a pole fixed to a yoke which the beasts keep up. The tail is simply a large branch roughly hewn and bent a little to form a handle; the share is of wood, with two side-pieces also of wood, bound by means of leathern thongs and with an iron tip in front. The men seem to till the land with great care, breaking the clods with a wooden mallet, and picking up the stones, which they place in a heap at the corner of the field. We see several others ploughing in the same way; the driver is sometimes a woman, but it is always a man with body bared who holds the tail and guides the plough lightly through the soil.

Turning to the lama-house, we see much more movement within it than there was yesterday. The dilapidations in the roof and walls are being repaired. Women carry the mortar and stones in baskets, while the men arrange the materials, and we see several of them treading the soil down on the roof and singing as they work. The lamas, richly clad, stand out boldly against the sky on the highest point of the roof, as they interest themselves in the work, and in various striking attitudes watch the men. These hurried repairs suggest that the rainy season is at hand.

April 16.—We quit So after having said our adieus to our companions, the minor chiefs, who are returning home. One of them is going to Lhassa, and we commission him to carry our kind remembrances to our old friends who live in the holy city.

Crossing the So-tchou, which here is from 480 to 660 feet broad, we have an involuntary bath. We then ascend a valley from which one of the tributaries of the So-tchou comes down. As we follow the banks of the river along an easy road with the sun shining brightly, our eyes are gladdened by the juniper and brushwood which cover the slopes on the higher ground; herds are browsing the green grass; yaks, sheep, and horses vie with each other in perching themselves on the most inaccessible spots. Every now and again black tents are to be seen in a gorge, and

A HOUSE AT SO.

near them blocks of ice, reminding us that the winter is only now over. In fact, we are perspiring, and have already forgotten the awful cold of the tablelands. At the end of the valley tents are pitched ready for us, with piles of faggots, and scarcely have we sat down when an old fellow presents himself with pendent tongue and a pot of creamy milk. Here we shoot some partridges that are quite new to us, and have been for a long time puzzling us by a cry which they uttered without showing themselves.

While searching for them I catch sight of three natives at our feet behind a rock, amusing themselves with the contemplation of their own features in a pocket mirror, which they are evidently using for the first time. They stop here for some time, chatting, and laughing boisterously at their own grimaces. The mildness of the temperature seems to us extraordinary; we no longer require our cloaks except after sunset. We again notice a curious phenomenon, though it is less striking here than on the tablelands: our woollen cloaks and clothes, whenever they are touched in the dark, become luminous with electricity, and give forth a slight crackle.

April 17.—Our road becomes more and more picturesque. We traverse regular woods of juniper trees, above which the green hills appear. Herds become more numerous, and trees more sparse. The method of building is no longer the same, for other materials are here available. We see huts, made of branches, built against the mountain-side, and the tents are surrounded with hedges, as among the Kirghis on the mountains of Central Asia, while the animals are shut in at night, because of the cultivated lands. Fires are made of wood, with which dung is mixed. The men are also laying by supplies of grass for the winter, and everywhere we see erections that look like gallows or gibbets, formed of upright poles, on the tops of which others are fixed crosswise; on these they dry the grass, which is, at the same time, out of reach of the cattle. In proportion as the land is more generous, the inhabitants take more care of themselves, and have stronger frames. For the first time we notice among these shepherds the use of a covering other than the cloak, for some are wearing cotton shirts with broad sleeves, and others sleeveless waistcoats. Almost all of them smoke pipes of tin or beaten iron, with tubes so long that by slightly stooping the smoker can light his very bad tobacco at the fire. On the road they carry, attached to their tobacco-pouch, a little wooden vessel in which they empty the residue of each pipe, and quickly filling the small bowl, light the fresh tobacco from the burning remains.

At Souti, in the valley of Soudjou, we were as astonished to see a man with a little black beard as we are at home to see a woman with hair on her chin. This individual, adorned also with a rudimentary moustache, is in other respects very like his fellows. He seems to be in the service of the local chief, who attracts our attention at once, for he seems an exact picture of what a barbarian chief should be. No longer young, for his hair is turning grey, he is still active and vigorous; his style of salutation is dignified though simple; he has regular features, thin lips, small eyes, with a proud look in them, and in all his gestures there is a certain amount of distinction combined with simplicity and ease. Whether he is walking, lighting his pipe—which is as long as his arm—or resting, he looks well. Ask him a question and he replies seriously; he issues brief orders that are quickly executed. He commands in a natural way, like a man born to be obeyed.

Since leaving So, we have often noticed that the soil on the banks of the river has been disturbed. To-day the mystery is solved, for on the fire near the tent we see a pot filled with what seems to be, from its taste, a kind of turnip. It is called *niouma*, and is found in the ground, just like truffles, growing generally with a long root, in which case it has a flat top like a mushroom, but sometimes the root is short.

From Souti we reach Ritchimbo by a pass, and are scarcely in the valley before we meet with an easterly wind, for the first time these many weeks, and a storm of sleet. The juniper trees have almost entirely disappeared, and here we are on a steppe again.

We have to change our yaks to-day, and for the last time we pay our workmen and drivers directly for their services. They always hand their money at once to their chiefs, who appropriate two-thirds of it, under the idea, doubtless, that we are "ruining trade." For the future, we shall simply hand a lump sum to the chief of the band, taking care to be less generous. We have often asked each other why savages submit so readily to the extortions of their chiefs. An Oriental gave us an explanation of this which may be worth mentioning. "We greatly prefer dishonest chiefs," said he, "because they punish us less severely when we deserve punishment, and we can obtain from them favours which it would be useless to ask from honest chiefs, who refuse bribes. The latter only do and permit what is just and right."

At Ritchimbo we see, for the first time, a goitre, on the neck of a small chief.

April 20.—The whole mountain is covered to a depth of about four inches with fine snow, which began to fall last night. After climbing a very difficult pass, called Kela, which is also the name of the neighbouring chain, and reaching, with great trouble and in intolerable heat, a height of 15,200 feet, the descent began. The snow was positively dazzling in the sunshine, and our faces were scorched, for we could not protect ourselves against the reflection of the sun's rays, after the manner of the natives, who let their long hair hang down over their faces. They, however, suffer from headache, to relieve which they put handfuls of snow on their heads. It took us three hours to cross the pass, and we then followed the course of a river, sometimes on the ice and sometimes on the bank. On the adjacent lands were houses with flat tops, and surrounded with hedges; dogs greeted us with their barking, and we fancied we could even hear cats mewing, though it might, perhaps, have been little lambs bleating. Juniper trees were again very scarce, but the hill-sides bristled with brushwood; and every time that we raised our eyes we saw yaks where one would think only birds could perch. Then, leaving the valley, we climbed a ridge which forced us to go out of our way, with the result that we stumbled along towards a chief's house near Bata-Soumdo. This place, we are told, is on Chinese territory; it is near a training-school for lamas situated on the west side of the valley, which looks from here like a *cul-de-sac*, stretching from north to south, and shut in on the north by a superb mass of bristling broken rocks, with their slim and snowy points rising one above the other. The whole looks like an immense assemblage of tapering Gothic spires. On this side are more houses built on and round the slopes, while above and below cattle are grazing.

Our approach causes considerable curiosity, and several women, freshly besmeared, come out of the house. One of them is young, and as she does not wear a mask of dirt, displays fine features and a prepossessing face set in a natural head of hair, curly beyond all description. This head of hair is evidently "inhabited," but, from the calm fashion in which she disposes of those of her little six-footed friends that she can catch, it does not seem to enter her mind that she is at all singular in this respect. The chief, who is a fearful old rascal and very ugly, makes a difficulty about supplying us with yaks and horses, though we offer to pay him for their use. He pretends that he has none at his disposal. We can see plenty of them on the mountain, however, and call his attention to this manifest contradiction, and, being thus cornered, he avows that he can do nothing on his own authority. "I must," he says, "have an order from the Chinese chief at Lhassa or Tsiamdo. Have you one?" Thereupon our lama and the representative of the chief at So take him in hand, and the affair is soon settled. We express our astonishment at this difficulty, and our lama explains to us that the people in this valley are brigands, thieves, blackguards, in short, Chinese subjects, and that they are dependent on the Chinese mandarins at Tsiamdo.

Our afternoon is devoted to a reception of crowds of idlers whom we allow to inspect our various utensils. Some enamelled dishes call forth expressions of great admiration, while they raise their thumbs at the sight of our firearms, and greet our big-tailed ram with shouts of joy.

By dint of small presents, we induce some of the yak-drivers from Ritchimbo to transport our baggage during the four days that we have still to pass on the territory of Tsiamdo. The most ardent advocate in our behalf is a kind of idiot, about fifty years old, whom his comrades obey in spite of his evident lack of intelligence. We secured his allegiance by giving him a pocket mirror, which he had asked for scores of times during the stage. Although so simple-minded, he has wonderful legs, and is never tired of using them. On the slightest excuse he would come up to us, and hold the horse's bridle, under the pretence of being of some assistance; and, hanging out his tongue, would pretend to look at himself in the hollow of his hand, as if he were holding a looking-glass in it, and with the gestures and mimicry of a Neapolitan would beg us to give him one. Since our arrival at Bata-Soumdo he has never ceased hanging about Rachmed, whom he knows to be the cashier, the dispenser of our goods; and when Dedeken hands him the longed-for mirror, he receives it with an amusing explosion of joy that we have never seen equalled. Raising his arms, he looks at himself, protrudes his tongue, and gives a bound in the air, kicking up his heels. He then runs to the women, and allows them to contemplate their own features in his glass, but repulses them roughly when they try to take it into their own hands. Some men then approach, whereupon he runs away with a bound like a goat that has just been let loose, pursued by some of his companions, who cannot catch him up. He then stops, and allows them just a glance at themselves in his glass, but that is all, and at last he conceals this precious object, and each time that anyone asks him for the loan of it, replies, in a serious tone, that they have had enough amusement for the present. This strange man marks his friendship for a certain little girl by handing her a little bit of glass off a box of cigarettes; and she immediately holds this glass in the palms of her hands, and contemplates her reflected image, all the women following her example.

April 21.—We start, though rather late, to-day, for we have been obliged to adopt persuasive measures to induce a very recalcitrant chief to furnish us with his quota of men and beasts. Our lama and Rachmed at last bring him to understand that we distribute with no sparing hand blows as well as more agreeable things.

WOMEN AT BATA-SOUMDO.

CHAPTER XIII.

NATIVE CUSTOMS AND CHARACTER.

A Thibetan Vitellius—*Tchang*—Commercial Chinamen—Native Women—Polyandry and Polygamy—Beggars—Contentment—The Chief of the District at Home—A Theological Question—Departure from Sérésumdo—Mendicant Lamas and their Music—News from Lhassa—The Honeymoon in Thibet—Novel Method of Crossing a Stream—Tumblers—A Chief in His Cups—A Scene of Home Life—*Force Majeure*—Fickleness of the Natives: The Probable Cause—At Karimeta—Primitive Husbandry—A Lamaess—Praying Windmills—Tchoungo—The Dâla and Djala Passes—A Splendid Prospect—A Pagoda—Houmda—Lagoun: a Manufacturing Town.

WOMAN AND CHILD OF SÉRÉSUMDO.

April 21.—We make a short stage as far as Poioundo, half-way through a pass. The slopes are covered with brushwood, and in a thicket of rhododendrons we can see musk-deer bounding about. Some natives are very anxious to sell us musk-bags, and, to prove their generosity, offer us, at the same time, some of the long teeth of these animals. But these cunning salesmen, who ask at least twenty-five rupees apiece for the bags, are regular cheats, for they have emptied most of the bags and crammed them with paper.

April 22.—We traverse several short passes marked by *obos*, from which protrude branches tied up in bundles. We mount to a height of 16,500 feet, then descend, to mount again to a height of 15,500 feet; then there come passes of only 13,900 feet, and 14,900 feet. Now and again we see houses and tents on the plateau; around us is the fresh grass; and our temperature at night varies from 7° to 25° below zero.

April 23.—A pretty steep pass takes us up to a height of

15,000 feet, and then comes a descent into a narrow gorge rendered very picturesque by rocks, gradually broadening into a valley, while on the terraces above its perpendicular banks are numerous flat-roofed habitations with grey walls varying in height.

HOUSE AT SÉRÉSUMDO.

A large square building which frowns down upon them in the distance gives these houses the appearance of forts surmounted by a tower, such as are found in Tuscany.

Just as we were about to leave the valley, our old friend the idiot with the looking-glass rushed forward, and explained to us, with great volubility and gesticulations, that we were to halt on the plateau: "A grand chief, a very good fellow, is expecting you. I have told him that you are honest, kind men, and that you must make each other's acquaintance, and drink a glass of *tchang* together; you will find it excellent." We had no sooner reached the platform, which borders a river of considerable width, than we saw a number of natives who seemed to be expecting us. Several of them came forward, and, politely taking our horses by their bridles, conducted us to this great chief, who was one of the stoutest, if not the very stoutest, of Thibetans that we had ever seen—quite a Vitellius. In spite, or perhaps because of, his rotundity, he was very amiable, shaking our hands most cordially, and begging us to honour him by taking a seat on his rug. On each side of him was a lama, one with a head like an actor, the other with that of a faun. He himself carried on his bull-neck a splendid, well-shaped head—the head of a savage monarch, with hair hanging down his back. This specimen of a thick-set Goliath insisted on our tasting the contents of three iron bottles, cased in tin, of Chinese make, judging by their shape; on the liquid, lumps of butter were floating, having been added to the decoction out of compliment to us. From its flavour, this *tchang* must be made from fermented barley, and at first we did not think much of it, but after a while we rather took to it, and gave it the high-sounding name of hydromel. It seems very mild, but if you drink too much of it you run the risk of becoming "dead drunk." Our host requested permission to look at our firearms and glasses, and his stupefaction was extreme when he saw the dust fly, a thousand paces off, where a ball had struck a heap of rubbish on a rock; his companions sharing his astonishment, and expressing their admiration in most emphatic terms. When we rose to leave, the fat chief and all his followers insisted on conducting us, so they brought him a splendid mule, which, in spite of his weight, he mounted unaided; and so we started. Having crossed the river, our crowd of followers on foot tucking up their clothes and displaying the sturdy though somewhat long legs of mountaineers, we climbed a narrow path on the edge of the chasm, pitching our tent near a clump of houses built on the mountain-side. A crowd of idlers of both sexes soon surrounded us; the women being very ugly, while a few of the young men had rather nice faces.

To our yak-drivers, and all these spectators who are shouting and moving about, two Chinamen with their solemn mien present a great contrast. One of them wears a pair of spectacles with rims so large that they cover part of his forehead. He is smoking a cigar out of a long mouthpiece with a very dignified air, one hand in his girdle. The other, whose nose is not quite so insolently *retroussé*, has a less dignified attitude, and a humorous smile. They enter at once into conversation with our man Akoun, who turns out to come from Ken Si, their native province. Chinamen who belong to the same district always support each other, and when far from home meet compatriots with the greatest pleasure, their provincialism doing duty for patriotism.

These two are here to trade, and are the scouts of an army of invading merchants. They buy musk chiefly, or rather take it in exchange for tea, which they bring from China, a tea of a very inferior quality, furnishing, indeed, an execrable drink; yet the natives here prefer it to anything else, even to Indian rupees. According to these Chinamen, musk is very dear, a good bag costing at least twenty rupees. The natives also exchange it for tobacco, but only on rare occasions, as the tobacco-leaves, which they roll into cigars for themselves, come from Setchoun, and are very expensive.

According to what the elder and graver of the Chinamen tells us, they are both representatives of a large house, whose headquarters are at Shanghai. "My companion," he says, "was a soldier, and has travelled in the direction of Yunnan. I am going away from here in three hours, but he will remain, as he has come to take my place. My residence here has lasted eighteen months, and it will procure me, on my return home, the post of manager of one of the shops belonging to our house. Oh! you might be kind enough to let me have one of your horses. I noticed that one of them is lame; let me have it, and I will soon set it to rights. I should be very glad of it, for I want it badly."

"What do you want it for?"

"Because, you see, I have a little daughter whom I wish to take away with me, and I could put her on your horse."

"Are you not taking the child's mother, too?"

"No, for I am not married."

Thereupon his companion, the old soldier, also unbosoms himself to us. "I only arrived here three moons ago, and it already seems a very long time to me. I don't like being here at all, and I shall never be able to take to these savages or learn their language." He calls our attention to their dirt, though that does not prevent him from leering at some fearful-looking women. He is evidently a "lady's man," but, as he himself remarks, they are not by any means coy; they are indeed devoid of all sense of modesty or even of decency.

The poorer women adorn themselves with copper bracelets and earrings, the rich have silver ones. Many of them wear glass necklaces which they buy from the Chinamen, and stones among which agates predominate. They also insert these stones and glass trinkets in their abundant locks, which fall like a fan down their backs. Most of the women whom we see here have small dark eyes, black hair, broad faces, and prominent cheekbones; they are stout and short, but very strong and muscular. We are in a land where the system not only of "wives many," but also of "husbands many" prevails. This is how the latter mode works. A couple have a marriageable daughter; a man is anxious to enter into this family, live under the same roof, and become the husband of the girl. He therefore visits her parents, states the terms he is prepared to offer, and when this dowry—or, rather, this charge for admission—is settled, becomes her husband and a member of the family. Other young men, desirous of sharing his happiness, present themselves, knock at the door, and, if terms can be arranged, take their place, too, around the family hearth, thus becoming members of the household and co-husbands. Sometimes, but very rarely, it happens that one of the husbands, through love or jealousy, or from some other motive, wishes to become the sole proprietor, the sole lord of the wife.

TYPES OF NATIVES AT SÉRÉSUMDO.

In this case terms are arranged by which he becomes her sole master, and his colleagues obligingly retire, when he has repaid them the sum they brought on entering the association, plus an indemnity, the amount of which is only settled after a long wrangle. If there are any children, they remain with the wife.

It must not be imagined that this system prevails by law or by any religious custom having the force of a law. In Thibet polyandry is not obligatory, as monogamy is with us. If his means admit of such a luxury, a man takes a wife to himself and does not share her with others. And if a powerful, rich chief, like the great man who welcomed us this morning, is not content with one wife, he takes as many as he likes. Our Goliath, for instance, has three, so that this country furnishes a proof, as do other countries, that polyandry and polygamy are determined by economic considerations.

Let me give another fact in support of this view. A married man gives up his wife, and restores her to her family, when he finds "double harness" too galling. He can, if he chooses, enter a lama-house, a favour, however, that is granted him only in return for a certain sum paid down into the prior's hands. On becoming a lama, he is assured against want to the end of his days, a sort of life annuity being granted to him in exchange for his capital handed over to the house. His position, however, in the community is in proportion to his fortune; and should he be comparatively poor, he must not expect the happy and easy lot of the richer lamas, but must work. Even with this obligation to work, however, he is relatively happy, since his future is secure; he will never be without a crust to munch, and many of the natives are quite content when this much is assured to them.

Here, however, as elsewhere, some women are left unmarried. When they cannot find a purchaser their only resource is to take to begging; they soon meet with others in the same plight, with whom they join their fortunes, and they then wander about among tents and villages with wallets on their backs, and long sticks in their hands to repel the dogs. Sometimes they join a body of male beggars, when each sex begs for itself by day, and they only meet at night.

If it be asked, "When a woman has, say, four husbands, how can they possibly agree amongst themselves?" I can only assert that they do agree. They all, indeed, join hands against the wife. They vie with one another in getting as much work out of her as they possibly can. She it is who leads the yaks yoked to the plough, or, bare to the waist, brandishes a mallet as she breaks the clods; before sunset she hastens to the fields to collect fuel for the evening meal, and sometimes has to go, with her basket on her back, to the summit of the mountains, along the slopes, to gather it. If the stones in the walls that protect the cultivated lands fall down, she has to put them back again; it is she, too, who removes the stones turned up by the plough; she spins and sews, and attends to the heads of young and old; goes to the river for water, and, bending double on the steep path, returns laboriously with her jars full; while finally, when beasts of burden run short, or these "gentlemen" think a load too heavy for their little horses, they quietly put it on a woman's back. The women belonging to the nomads, however, are not so overdone with work as the wives of the husbandmen.

As for the men, they plough, sow, shoot, drive the yaks, and, with the help of their women, load them, but their chief occupation consists in smoking their pipes while waiting for the harvest.

All, however, women as well as men, seem quite contented with their lot, and gaiety reigns supreme. Every time they see us performing our ablutions they gape with astonishment. Our matches, too, fill them with amazement when they see them light from friction. Several of them rush to pick up those we have thrown away after using them, or because they would not strike. Then they rub them, just as they have seen us doing, on a stone or on their sleeves, and are crestfallen because they cannot produce the desired effect.

In the evening I took a walk in the direction of a large *obo* piled up at the bottom of a terrace where the chief of the district has built his palace. I found him before his door, sitting cross-legged on a mat in a very dignified position, and turning his prayer-mill. The suspicion of a beard and of a small black moustache, and his hair, which falls down only to his shoulders, make him the type of a Gallic chief as represented to us in pictures. Chained up in his yard are two splendid black dogs with red paws, enormous beasts with heads like bears, that bark furiously when anyone approaches.

The dwelling-house comprises the floor above the stables, and is reached by stairs, or rather by a trunk of a tree hewn into the shape of stairs. Between the first floor and the stables is a platform, on the walls of which hang fox, wolf, and panther skins. Women are attending to their household duties, while their lord and master is enjoying the fresh air. While I am examining some engraved stones, I am joined by a young lama, whose hooked nose, energetic features, and quick eye, had already struck me. He presents me with several stones, saying, "I engraved the prayers on them." I compliment him on his talent, and express a wish to carry away with me some specimens of his skill, whereupon he shows himself disposed to fall in with my request, and taking my note-book, which I hand him, copies into it some of the inscriptions.

We were soon surrounded by idlers, and among them were some lamas who read aloud over his shoulder the formulæ which he was copying for me. Then one of them, to whom I remarked that the words were very beautiful, put a question to me, folding his hands in the attitude of prayer, affecting to turn his prayer-mill to the right, and pointing to the south and to the lama's house on the other side of the valley opposite to us. He next pretended to turn a prayer-mill to the left, and pointed to the west, namely, the direction of Lhassa. He was doubtless putting to me a question in theology, or perhaps he wanted to know my opinion on Buddhism. Being an old hand at this kind of thing, I pointed to the west and turned my imaginary mill from right to

MENDICANT LAMAS (p. 132).

left, and, lifting my thumb, expressed my approbation of this latter kind of exercise. It so happened that I was of the scribe's opinion, for he congratulated me, repeating with manifest satisfaction, " Well, very well ! "

After that he made some jocose remark to my questioner, who

is doubtless an innovator or schismatic of some kind. He has, however, a good round head, and a benevolent face, which does not look as though it belonged to a revolutionist. With a firm hand the artist wrote the "Om mané Padmé houm," then "Ome ma té me ie sa le deu," and then other syllables, the significance of which I will not undertake to furnish. It is, however, to be supposed that they have a meaning, and that they are efficacious, since they are everywhere chiselled on stones, chalked on mountain-sides, traced on the shingle of the river, printed on the stuffs, or cut on bits of wood, and even on the animals' horns when other material fails. In reward for his kindness I handed the scribe the pencil he had been using. As he had picked up all the bits of old paper that we had thrown away, he drew out of his pocket a bit of an old cardboard box, and had a hard tussle with the point of the pencil, writing in cursive characters, and drawing ornaments, a hand, a bird that looks like an indiscriminate specimen of a domestic fowl, and finally my portrait, consisting of a very short profile, with what was meant for a nose, an eye like that of an Egyptian, narrow forehead, and a beard such as you see on Assyrian bas-reliefs.

The likeness was not satisfactory, but I, in turn, executed his portrait, reproducing his aquiline nose and advancing chin. It really was recognisable; at all events, he was so pleased with it that, when he asked to be allowed to retain this masterpiece, I consented, and he took his departure surrounded by his friends, who, on comparing the drawing with its original, raised their thumbs to compliment me on my talent.

April 24.—To-day we left Sérésumdo, although we had been very comfortable there. Before starting, the chief offered us several bottles of *tchang*, which we emptied, making a merry start, accompanied by most of the villagers.

The valley that we now ascend is well cultivated, with numerous hamlets in it, and large farms where all the members of a family are crowded together. The ruins of habitations surmounted by lofty towers are not rare. We could not find out whether these *despobladas* were due to war, depopulation, or removals. Built on elevated platforms, bathed in the sunshine, and standing out against the blue sky, these towers have an imposing aspect, and give to the ruins the appearance of fortified castles. The buildings correspond in style with those I have seen on the Himalayas, in the Tchatral, and at Gahkoush, for instance. There are resemblances, also, between the natives of these two regions—the same long hair, the same system of one wife to several husbands, the same easy carrying of heavy loads, and, finally, the same lightheartedness.

After advancing for an hour and a quarter, we halted at a small village to change porters. From the moment of our arrival the chief from Sérésumdo, who had accompanied us, sat apart to show that he does not exercise any authority here, and that he will not interfere in his neighbours' concerns. These little potentates are, in fact, very jealous of their authority. The chief, who is recognisable by his yellow, pointed hat, marches up and down, and issues his orders, his men forthwith setting out in every direction, shouting, calling, and answering one another till the mountain echoes back the noise. They bring up beasts of burden of every sort, size, and colour, male and female. One drags a donkey by its ear, another a yak by a cord or by its horn, others chase horses, an old woman hurries on her cow, and some young men drive-in oxen at a gallop; all these make up a large herd, and they add their lowing, grunting, or neighing to the hubbub, which was bad enough before. When it comes to starting, and dividing the loads, there is a general scramble for the lightest objects, men and women, old men and children, all taking part in it, and all arguing. They weigh the chests and the bundles, and all want to get out of taking them. One pretends that his ass is so miserably small; another, that he cannot saddle his horse because it is too spirited; another, that his yak has only just come in, tired out from ploughing; and as for our wild-yak skin, destined for the Museum, they are so frightened at its weight that no one will have anything to do with it. Everybody is crying out, everyone issuing orders, down to boys of twelve, while, amid all the tumult, some sanctimonious old lamas, quite indifferent to it, quietly turn their mills or tell their beads. But this does not prevent them from examining us and stroking our velveteens, which are a puzzle to them; as they feel them, they remark to each other, "It is not leather," and they cannot get over their surprise. The shouting and laughing are enough to deafen one. Soon the din is at its height, thanks to the arrival of two mendicant lamas singing, the one in a marvellously hollow voice, the other in tones first sharp and then rough. They accompany their song with a double tambourine, which they beat till the little leather tassels flutter at the end of the thongs attached to the instrument. Besides this, they every now and then blow into human thigh-bones with leather bags at the end, from which most disagreeable wheezing noises proceed. Both of the men are bare-headed, and clad in yellow; the elder one's face is completely smooth; the other is bald, his nose is short, his teeth are excellent, and he possesses just a large enough fringe of beard to make him the image of a good-natured gorilla.

The scene is a picturesque one, and it would probably be going on still if the chief, tired of arguing with his subjects, had not suggested to them that they should decide by lot who should take such and such a load. Men and women accordingly hand to an old man one of the garters with which they fasten up their stuff boots above the calf. These form the numbers of the lottery, and the old man proceeds to draw them with the utmost impartiality. He first places himself at one end of the row of packages, and, following it down to the other end, puts upon each of them one of the garters which he takes at haphazard out of his left hand, kept behind his back. Two sturdy fellows having voluntarily seized the heaviest chests, the crowd straightway lays hold of all that is left, and our baggage is soon carried off.

Everyone wishes to join in this pleasure party, poor as well as rich, the women more especially; and the exodus takes place in great disorder, while those who carry small loads, or none at all, run about, jumping round the beasts, laughing, chattering, and shouting; never, in short, did a "removal" take place amid greater merriment.

In our turn we followed this rabble, after having given a consultation to one of the mendicant lamas, who had an eye covered with a white film. On the way we noticed that our yak-skin, which, at starting, had been put on a young horse, had found its way to the shoulders of a woman, so important is it that the back of the noblest conquest that man has ever made should not be made sore. In spite of the impossibility of overlooking our porters, we found in the evening that nothing was missing.

Scarcely was our tent pitched, when our Chinaman was greeted by a Thibetan with an intelligent face, who could speak a few words of Chinese. He represented that he came from Lhassa, and that he was there while we were at Dam, for the rumour of our arrival had spread in the town. He had three other companions, one of them a girl, and they had been travelling for a year. Setting out from Tatsien-Lou, whither they were now returning, they passed Tsiamdo, and then went straight to Lhassa, to pray and receive the blessing of the Talai-Lama.

"And did you receive it?"

"Oh, yes! we were blessed, and are now happy. As soon as we have reached home again, my sister is going to marry the elder of these two young men."

"And who is the other?"

"The brother of her future husband."

"Your brother-in-law is very young."

"Eighteen."

"And your sister?"

"Fifteen."

"What induced you to undertake this long journey?"

"We had long talked about it between us, and then, when we had made up our minds, we set out with a little money. Now, however, we have none left, and are begging our way back."

"Do you expect to reach Tatsien-Lou soon?"

"We hope so, but cannot say when."

In Europe the honeymoon trip is made after marriage; in Thibet they take it at betrothal. I will not presume to decide which of the two plans is the better.

In front of our encampment, on a plateau to the south, stretch the white walls of a lama's house, from which the descent is made by an abrupt path cut in the high bank of the river. The two banks are not connected by any bridge, and those who would cross must do so at a ford, or make use of a cable stretched above the water from side to side.

On going to examine this system of aërial gymnastics, we were lucky enough to see it work several times. The person who crosses encircles his body with short leather thongs attached to a strong horn hook, which is fixed over the stomach. Then with the ends of these thongs he forms two rings, which are passed round the thighs, hangs the hook on to the rope, with the heads in the direction he is going, and holding on by his wrist, is soon suspended, face uppermost and back parallel to the river, when he soon twists himself over to the other side. Several natives who crossed to have a look at us returned in this manner; each had his straps and his hook, while those who felt their strength going nerved themselves by shouting, and pressed the cord with their feet, besides pushing themselves along by stretching their legs. Some of them displayed great strength in this exercise, and when hanging in mid-air over the river which was roaring beneath them, would give vent to shouts of joy or defiance.

In the evening three Thibetans came and took a seat round our fire, one of them twanging a guitar as an accompaniment to a song which, though monotonous, was not disagreeable. The following evening, when the beasts were being loaded, they reappeared in their smartest costume, having tucked their trousers into their boots, and put on a red dress with tassels hanging down from their girdles.

These men are dancers or tumblers. Winding round in a circle, they mark time with small cymbals and a drum, which they hold like a hand-glass and strike with a bent stick, with a leather puff at the end. They make a few grimaces, bend the body, and then with great agility turn clean over. As a climax, one who remained on the scene last added to his disguise a horrible-looking mask, ornamented with white shells, and performed a series of leaps and somersaults, which he made more dangerous by holding close to his eyes the points of very sharp knives.

April 25.—We mounted up as far as Tachiline, crossing to the left bank of the river by a wooden bridge. The piles are square towers, constructed of small beams, and the interiors filled with stones. On the top of these piles long oak beams are put, fixed with ropes to cross-beams, and having stones on the ends to keep them in position, and, perhaps, to maintain the equilibrium.

Here we had to consult the chiefs of the district about obtaining yaks for the next stage, which is a long one, beginning with a pass, and continuing through a desert, so we were asked to start early. The head of the lama-house helped us, and half our band for the morrow will consist of lamas. There are two hundred of them here, living in a row of huts so out of repair that we can only conclude it is a poor district—and, in fact, the natives cultivate very little ground, and are smaller and worse off than those who live lower down. In ten hours we reached Tchimbo-Tinzi, a large village with a lama community numbering a thousand inhabitants. It is perched on an isolated shelving road, and bordered on the south by the river, which buries itself in a ravine, to the north being a valley which supports the whole population.

The chief is at variance with a neighbour, who wishes to take advantage of his minority to invade his territories. But though the young chief, by the advice of the old men, resists, he will one day succumb, for the Chinese authorities at Tsiamdo have been subsidised by the ambitious chief of Tchimbo-Nara, and they will interfere in his favour with a view to weakening the power of our host.

April 26.—We saw the ambitious chief to-day. We had, however, to wait a very long time for him in the valley, his village being perched high up like an eagle's nest, and he himself being quite tipsy. As soon as he had recovered the use of his legs, he descended from his eyrie. He proved to be an enormous fellow, with grey eyes; but was pleasant in his cups, giving his orders with great decision, and setting everybody to work. The required number of yaks were soon got together, the great chief spending his leisure moments in drinking astride across a bale, looking like a clumsy Silenus. Every now and then there issued from his ponderous bosom shouts with which the whole valley resounded, and which were the outcome of his great animal spirits. We left him with mutual expressions of goodwill, after having bought a sheep from him for two shillings.

Hamlets and farms abound hereabouts, built of rough stones, the terraces and roofs resting on trunks of trees. We are still in

SCENE NEAR SÉRÉSUMDO.

a wild district, but the natives live in houses, and there are signs of the early stage of civilisation. They till their land better, and manure their fields, they wear stuff clothes, and nearly all their women adorn themselves with glass trinkets; their hair is shorter, and they often wear it level with the shoulder, while the women cut theirs over their forehead into a fringe, and do not wear it down their backs in little plaits. Armed men are much rarer, as if there were greater security than in the districts situated to the west.

To-day, after having, by a mistake, left the banks of the river, we followed a path which led us to a farm, where we came across a scene of Thibetan home life. In the yard, a man, bare to the waist, is skinning a sheep on the ground; a child of eight or nine is holding it by the paws, and, as he bends down, his head is completely hidden by his falling hair. The dogs are eagerly awaiting the moment when the uneatable portions will be flung to them. Seated on a stone and leaning against the wall, a handsome young woman, with bare neck and chest, is holding a distaff and spinning, in a calm attitude; at her feet is a little girl, drawing out the wool. A man seated at her side is conversing smilingly with her; another, with bare body, who is sharpening a blade on a stone, has his arms stretched out in the pose of the antique knife-grinder to be seen at Florence. A plump little girl is playing with a puppy which has about as much clothing as herself. Lower down, out in the sunshine, an old woman, with her short white hair all in disorder, is lolling over a few cinders, enjoying the short span of life that remains to her. By her side sleeps a very old dog, toothless and mangy, his muzzle resting on his wasted old paws; like his mistress, he awaits death with the blue sky above him.

At Gratou we found ourselves amongst very unsociable people, from whom it seemed utterly impossible to purchase even a goat or a sheep. We now regretted that we had no dogs; for we left one behind us, a second was killed, while the third, a good watch-dog, has not been trained to catch and strangle sheep and goats, as the one that is dead had. As we could not induce these people to listen to reason—though a Mongolian lama, who joined us a few days ago and acts as our interpreter, tried in vain to persuade them to furnish us with meat—we attempted to seize some without permission. This brought upon Dedeken and Rachmed a shower of stones, and there were a few sharp-shooters posted on the roofs. A few revolver shots in the air, however, settled the matter.

It has often been, and doubtless often will be, our fate to have difficulties with these Thibetans. They have never seen any Europeans before, and do not know how to treat us; while, fickle to an extraordinary extent, a mere nothing changes their attitude. They shift from the most abject submission to the most audacious insolence; one moment with their foreheads on the ground, the next they are standing erect, sword in hand. It would seem as though fear were at the bottom of all their emotions. One alarm sets them in one direction, then another cause of fear sets them off in another, and so their feeble will vacillates, shifting like a needle between two poles. They prefer before everything else relaxation and sleep; and whether in order to be left quiet, or because they are put out with those who disturb them, they have outbursts of passion, like the man who killed the wolf by day because it frightened him by night.

Their heads must be crammed with superstition, for it would seem as though they regarded strangers as mysterious beings, whom it is imperative to distrust, for to have come from afar they must have used witchcraft. Having noticed that these savages welcome the gift of a coloured image, we distributed some among them at different times. A boy of fourteen or fifteen having approached us, I offered him one, with the result that he ran away. So I let it drop on the ground, whereupon he went up to it with great precaution, looking at it from a distance, but, when the colours caught his eye, drawing nearer to examine it. Then he again retreated, but his curiosity brought him back again, and he beckoned to an older lad. The latter, in turn, examined this curious object, bending down and picking it up, and then ran after me, with a view to handing it back. When I told him to keep it, he was delighted, but a lama, about twenty years old, then came up and spoke to him sharply as though to inspire him with disgust at his present. They consulted together for a moment, after which they proceeded to the stream, and left the image there.

By the evening the inhabitants had calmed down, and eagerly implored our Mongolian lama not to fulfil his threat to go to the lama-house to complain of having been struck.

April 28.—At early dawn the natives began to get ready for us all that we wanted, and a mere glance sufficed to put to flight the chief of those who gave us so much trouble yesterday. At Karimeta we pitch our tents at the doors of an extensive lama-house, and witness a curious sight. The lamas have engaged the women of the neighbouring villages to come and carry manure to their fields, for this red-soiled valley is carefully cultivated, and most of it belongs to them. They have just finished ploughing, and the soil has the pink tinge of flesh from which the outer skin has been peeled off. While the lamas, on the first floor of their monastery, are chanting their prayers to an accompaniment of tambourines and cymbals, more than fifty women are wending their way in and out from the stables to the fields, with osier baskets on their backs. These they fill with ashes and manure, and then, in single file, like ants carrying their provender, proceed to empty them, at the foot of a hill, in the newly ploughed furrows. There is very little method and a good deal of noise over the work, which is superintended by a lame lama, who has frequently to hasten the steps of these ladies, for they are so interested in us that they keep edging out of their path so as to get nearer to us, when they stop for a good look and chatter. But though he feels the responsibility of his post, the lame lama is not a whit less curious than they, and he, too, even while on the move, must look at us. This strong desire of his to do two things at a time affords us considerable amusement, for as one of his legs is much shorter than the other, he has to look at the ground each time he puts his foot down, but, in his anxiety to watch us, he then turns his head in our direction. As he goes through his various manœuvres, he looks exactly like a mechanical toy; marching along, telling the beads of a huge rosary, jerking forward his short leg, lowering and then raising his head, twisting it to the right, leaning to the left, crying " Forward!" to his workwomen, then hurriedly throwing out his arms to recover the equilibrium which he has lost by stumbling against a stone, shouting out again, and, in a word, tossing himself about in the most comical manner imaginable.

Among our female coolies is one whose close-shaven head indicates that she has renounced marriage and taken the vow of celibacy; she is a lamaess. Neither handsome nor pretty, very short and thick-set, she has a large head and brutish features; and there is not a spark of intelligence in her face. The crowd of basket-carriers arrives, chattering in the pleasing tones which come as such a surprise from such ugly throats; for these Thibetans are apes with the voices of nightingales. All of a sudden our lamaess runs towards the file of fuel-gatherers, and goes straight up to a friend of hers, another close-shaven lamaess. They smile and bow to each other until their foreheads touch, in the same manner that two goats butt each other, after which these two schoolfellows go along side by side gossiping.

Examining the house of the lamas, which, like all of its kind, is composed of cottages and small rooms in juxtaposition, with a large hall set apart for their idol and for worship, we observe their agricultural implements. First, there is a rake, made, like our mill-rakes, of a little board, shaped like a crescent, with a handle; then there is a pickaxe, consisting of a wooden cube, which is cut down to a point. The point is shod with an iron cone; and as that metal is scarce hereabouts, it is used sparingly. Another kind of pickaxe resembles that which we use for gardening, but the edge only is made of iron, the rest being of wood; and it has a long handle.

A layman is putting a thatch of barley-straw on the roofs of the cottages by means of a kind of double flail consisting of two switches, which are fastened together by a strap fixed to a handle. These switches serve to cut the straw into short bits, for it is not given to the cattle until it has undergone this preparation. Let me add that the people of Thibet are more careful about their cattle than about themselves. The horses, as well as the yaks which carry our baggage, are well treated, and fed in a very peculiar manner, with a kind of pap made with the *niouma* (a species of turnip), this food being put down their throats by means of a funnel made from a horn that has been hollowed out.

On the roof of this habitation of the lamas are windmills turning prayers, and likewise tridents of metal, which have led people to believe that Lamaism was derived from the worship of Neptune, the ruler of the waves. The little column supporting this trident is covered with stripes of black and white stuff. We also see a big T, surmounted by a crescent bearing on the concave side two spheres, placed one above the other. At one extremity of the bar of the T hangs a little bell.

At Karimeta we arranged, without much trouble, for our baggage to be carried to Tchoungo, which is situated above the river Tatchou. Tchoungo is a village of some importance, owing its reputation to the possession of an enormous *obo*, to walk round which at an ordinary pace takes three minutes. It is close to the house of a lama who is, so to speak, its guardian, and natives from the mountains are incessantly turning prayers around this pile, which they are careful to keep on their right side. Even very old people drag themselves slowly up to it, leaning on their crutches, in order to accomplish their devotions.

The weather is magnificent, and we have got down to 9,000 feet above sea-level, and at last are enjoying a summer temperature. The thermometer shows a maximum of 77° in the day-time, and at night it only goes as low as 26°.

After some difficulties with the authorities, whom we induced by threats to help us, we departed for the great lama settlement of Routchi. At first we ascended rising ground by following a picturesque gorge; in two hours reaching a smooth pass, upwards of 13,200 feet above the sea-level. It was a lovely bit of scenery; rocks, juniper trees, briars, rhododendrons, brush, and groves of fir-trees. On the steep bank of the river are some grottoes into which the water flows, while gigantic umbelliferous plants with stalks as thick as a man's wrist are numerous, and there were plenty of sparrows, curlews, and snipe.

May 7.—After a good night's rest we resumed our ascent on the 30th, and in two and a half hours arrived at the summit of the Dâla pass, 17,500 feet above the sea-level; while towards the south-west a great mountain chain with snow-covered peaks, from 19,800 to 21,500 feet high, is visible. Towards the north the mountains rise in terraces, undulating as far as the eye can see; they are of a greyish colour and free from snow. The general appearance suggests an ocean with its waves turned into stone—the long swell of a calm sea, as sailors call it.

The descent, or rather the "slide-down" on the snow, brought us once more to the desert, the slopes being bare, with here and there a few stunted junipers. In the valley of Dutchmé we found some tents pitched, and had to wait a whole day for a fresh relay of yaks, which had to be fetched from some distance. We

THE "OBO" AT TCHOUNGO (p. 18).

then followed the course of the rivers Détchou and Sétchou, and passing along the banks of the latter, traversed forests of fir trees. Piles of split wood were lying about, and we had some good sport with musk-deer and *crossoptilous*, a kind of white or slate-coloured pheasant, with which these woods swarm.

Then, when the Sétchou entered a gorge, we made for another pass, viz., the Djala, which is the name also of the whole mountain range. The Djala is 14,850 feet high; a stony path leads to the *obo*, near which we halted to give our cattle a rest. From this point the eye ranged over the finest bit of country that we had seen so far: the slopes at our feet were covered with fir trees, rhododendrons, and junipers of intense green; while higher up were grassy tablelands, dotted with herds of cattle, and near the crest, in the crannies, the snow was of a dazzling whiteness. It was not, however, nature which especially attracted our attention, but a piece of man's handiwork in the form of a pagoda. No better spot could have been found for this pagoda, built in a large square, rising in terraces, and serving, so to speak, as a pedestal for the column which towers like a golden flame towards the skies. Having lived, as we had done, for several months without seeing anything resembling a monument, we could easily imagine with what feelings the sight of such an edifice must inspire the uncivilised Thibetan, and what a grand notion he must form of the great lama who dwells in it. Now one can comprehend how great an influence architecture must exert upon the minds of men. It is evident that the Pharaohs, by placing their pyramids in the desert where they appear so huge, did not intend to keep the sands in their place, but to inspire mankind with respect and even adoration for those who had the power to raise up a mountain in the midst of grains of sand. Certain it is that the Thibetans have a profound veneration for this abode of the Talai-Lama. Do they see a symbol in the seven double stripes, painted in white upon the black walls of the edifice? Do they think at all, as they contemplate this pyramid, which seems to be made of gold and to terminate in a flame mingling with the skies? Do they see in that flame an allusion to the great soul that, according to Buddhism, permeates nature? Perhaps not; yet it cannot be doubted that the sight fills them with a mysterious awe.

By the side of the beautiful pagoda, which is reached by a wooden bridge, may be seen a lama-house, nestling against the mountain-side, with its many terraces of painted cottages. The village of the laymen is lower down; its low, box-like houses with flat roofs are crowded together in the peninsula of Routchi, which is washed by the river to the south, while breakwaters, formed by dovetailing the trunks of trees together, protect the banks from the current. In the village, yaks pass to and fro, dragging the stems of fir trees; for there is a considerable timber trade, from which the wealth of the lama-house is chiefly derived.

Leaving the village, we pass cows in the green meadows, and yaks wallowing in the ponds; the trees, as they are rolled down into the valley, make a noise like thunder. The path dips into the deep shade of the firs, the wind is gently swaying the slender twigs and sighing through the branches; the torrent-like Sétchou is beating against its steep banks. We have assuredly been transported into Switzerland, if not into the Himalayas.

The country is rich, compared with what we have seen before. The fields are protected by hedges made of interlaced fir branches; pieces of timber, fixed in the ground, enclose the pasture-lands where browse the herds which manure the soil, and where the sheep and goats are shut up on account of their destructive tendencies. Precautions are necessary, for the barley is showing its green blades, and the people are therefore repairing the hedges, or making new ones with green branches. These green branches will get dry, and in winter, when the ground is covered with snow instead of crops, will be used for firewood.

The houses are nearly always built in one style, with walls made of clods of earth and stones mixed, and flat roofs placed on branches. They are, however, surmounted by lattice-work for storing the fodder, which makes them look like buildings that have been abandoned when the first storey was being begun, and the scaffolding of which has been left standing.

To-day (the 7th) we reached Houmda, a village built on a shelving road made out of conglomerate, skirted on the eastern side by a torrent that empties itself into the Sétchou about 450 yards farther on. We found stationed there, on post and police duty, a company of Chinese soldiers, more or less stupefied by the use of opium. They sold us eggs at as high a price as they could extort from us, and were excessively polite. Most of them had been there for many years, and, having married Thibetan wives, had forgotten their own language. To their police duties they pay but very little attention, and brigands, if there are any, can carry on their operations with perfect security. In their exorbitant demands these Chinamen display an obsequiousness and a persistency that contrast greatly with the churlishness of many of the natives.

From Houmda the road would have taken us eastwards by Tsiamdo. On reflection we determined to avoid this populous town, which contains many Chinamen under the rule of a mandarin, for it would be difficult to get away if this official of the Celestial Empire should take it into his head to prove his power. Prudence, therefore, bids us make a *détour* over the mountains towards the north.

May 8.—To-day we visited Lagoun, a large industrial centre. The houses lie very near each other, and, after counting a score of them, we observed an unoccupied space, a sort of square on which wood was piled up. Then we entered into the chief's yard, where we were stared at by a number of idlers, amongst them several whose faces were blackened by smoke.

These were "hands" from the works, for Lagoun has a manufactory of all sorts of iron implements, hatchets, pickaxes, etc.

We visit this establishment, guided to it by the sound of hammers, to which we have long been strangers. By a low door we descend to an underground forge, four posts supporting the sloping roof by which the light enters and the smoke escapes. Someone is kneeling between two goatskin bellows which he works alternately with either arm. This old man is bare to the waist, and looks like a denizen of the lower regions. His body is almost transparent, his skin but parchment, his ribs protruding; while his head is like that of a corpse, and one long tooth is visible in his huge mouth. His scanty hairs drop like a mane, while from the shoulders hang, by way of arms, two fibreless feelers. Five or six young men are standing erect, silent, lean, consumptive, blackened, perhaps mummified, for they are motionless and speechless. And yet their dull eyes betray the fact that they are alive. The old man stops blowing, and, getting up, silently goes to a bag, fills a large wooden porringer with *zamba*, and sits down, the younger ones squatting round him, each producing his mug from the sheepskin hanging at his loins. The meal having been handed round, they pass a huge jug to the old man, who pours some water from it into his cup, the others following suit. Then, with hollowed hands, as black and as bony as claws, they slowly knead their quota, quite silent, and fixing on us six pairs of expressionless eyes.

We give the poor wretches a coin, which the old man takes with manifest stupefaction. Who ever gave him a present before? He looks at the rupee, feels it, turns it over, and having satisfied himself that it really is silver, casts two glances at his fellow-workmen as if to assure them that there is no deceit about it, and smiles, and they smile too. Putting down their cups, they thank us by raising their thumbs, and then set-to kneading their meal again.

Their tools are decidedly poor. We see some very short one-handed hammers; some with larger handles, two-handed ones; large shears for one or for two hands; a trough hewn out of the trunk of a tree contains the water in which they cool the iron; the forge is an earthenware trough in which burns charcoal that is enkindled by the bellows. By the side of the forge, half buried in the soil, is the trunk of a tree, in the stoutest part of which is a large bar of iron which does duty as an anvil. They also have boring machines, which consist of two bobbins with an interval between them, their one spindle being between two small horizontal planks, while the gimlet is beneath in an iron socket. These bobbins, of wood, are hollow, being filled with sand and filings, which are covered with skin; the rotary movement is produced by means of cross handles fitted to the lower part. Such is this den of native industry, the Creusot of Thibet, and its equipment.

PRAYER CARVED ON A STONE.

CHAPTER XIV.

FROM LAGOUN TO CHANGKA.

Lamé—Lamda—Bad Food—Religious Malthusianism—Crossing the Satchou—Capture of a New-born Monkey—Koushoune—Ouoshishoune—A Fat Lama—Dzérine—Hassar—Thibetans and Chinese: a Contrast—Indefinite Dates—Rough-and-Ready Justice—Dotou—A Dignified Chinese Official—A Series of Prayer Mills—Rachmed in Action—The Chinese Army—Parting with the Lama Guide—Tsonké—A Secret Christian—The Destruction of the Batang Mission—Burial-place of a French Missionary—Reception by the Mandarin of Changka—Four Swords for 150 Men.

THIBETAN OF TIÉCHOUNG.

May 8.—To-day we reached Lamé, a small village where the Chinese have a post of soldiers, some of whom can scarcely speak their mother-tongue. Two Thibetan chiefs came in due course to see us, and one of them, a fine-looking man of about forty, exchanged a few words with our lama, and went off again at once.

May 9.—We saw the chief again to-day at Lamda, on the banks of the Giometchou, the waters of which form, with the Satchou and the Zetchou, the river of Tchamdo which, much lower down, goes by the name of the Mekong. The Thibetan chief handed us a *cata* on behalf of his superior at Tsiamdo or Tchamdo, and told us we had only to express our wishes for them to be gratified. He added that it was difficult to procure provisions here, but that in two days' time we should be in a better position, and should receive as much rice, mutton, and flour as we required. It is easy to see, by the rapidity with which his orders are executed, that his authority in this region is unquestioned, and it is the first time since leaving So that we have found the natives so obedient to orders.

We reached Lamda over a pass 15,500 feet high, then descending through sunlit gorges, where mountain torrents

A THIBETAN VILLAGE.

bubbled and surged amid pleasant greenery. The heights are covered with rhododendrons, but lower down, amid the thickets formed of poplar, birch, and cherry-trees, one might fancy oneself in Europe. There is plenty of game, too, and we kill some splendid *ithagines* with red tails and green plumage, pheasants, etc., our collection being swollen by some new specimen every day.

May 13.—The weather has been magnificent, and on the night of the 9th the thermometer did not descend to freezing point. Batang is not far off, and the Thibetans are doing their best to redeem the promise they made at Dam to help us.

Nothing is wanting to make our comfort complete but a better supply of food, for although we have abundance so far as quantity goes, the rice is musty, the butter rank, the flesh of the goats execrable, and the pheasants stringy; only the Hodgson partridge being in the least toothsome. What we so long for is the day when we shall taste some good meat, vegetables, and fruits. Our tent is pitched at a spot which is at less than half the altitude of the point from which we started in the morning, and I amuse myself by watching a man and woman of the village whom we had employed to split some wood and fetch water, as they consume the remains of our supper, given them by Rachmed. They have taken off the pan in which the food was cooked, and the man, plunging the spoon into the mess, empties it on to his hand, and then jerks it into his mouth, looking at his companion as much as to say, "First-rate!" Then they take out the cups they carried in their bundles, fill them with rice and meat, and lap these up almost like water. They have never had such a good meal before.

At Lamda the Giometchou is about 150 feet broad, running along between rocks with a good deal of noise, and we cross it at the bridge of Sougomba, where there is a large dwelling-place for lamas built on the hill. If we were to continue our journey northwards, we should arrive at Sininfou, but after crossing the bridge, we turn round and encamp in a valley running down from the east to the Giometchou. Here, also, there is an abundance of game, including musk-deer, partridges, pheasants, and hares; and while the eastern slope of the mountains is thickly wooded, the western slope is nearly bare. From time to time we see hamlets which are rendered habitable by the water from the torrents being turned into the fields, through aqueducts hewn out of the trunks of trees. The houses are better built, the ground-floor, used for housing the stock, being made of stone with wooden doors, while the walls of the first storey are of mud.

Above are balustrades which are used as store-places; while if the house is built against a slope, there is often a second storey.

There are countless *obos*, and owing to the abundance of grass, the flocks and herds are very numerous; a fat goat or sheep costs two rupees.

We have scaled pass after pass, and to-day (the 13th) traversed the Ka-la, which is 15,500 feet high. We notice in this region that many of the people have their heads closely shaven, the tonsure indicating those who have been made to take a vow of celibacy from their childhood. It is said that, in former times, young children were offered to Moloch in order to appease him, and that they were placed inside his statue, which was then made red-hot, in order that he might consume them. Most of the males are now consecrated to Buddha, and the youth thus set apart do not marry, nor do they allow their hair to grow any more, and they wear a yellow garter on their leg. Owing to this system, families, as a rule, decline in number, and when the slightest epidemic occurs, they disappear, much to the satisfaction of the prolific Chinese.

This religious Malthusianism is calculated to please economists who think that the world is really too small for mankind, and that there would soon be no place to lay one's head if people multiplied in conformity with the laws of Nature. But if they were to visit some of the waste places of the earth, they would come to a very different conclusion.

May 14.—We cross the Satchou with our caravan of thirty-three people—including sixteen women, seven men with long hair, and ten lamas—upon a raft made out of trunks of trees, this raft, which is paddled across by three men, being sixteen feet long by ten wide. The Satchou is very rapid at this point, running at a speed of nearly four miles an hour between high banks, and being from 270 to 330 feet broad. On the banks willows are growing, while in the woods are wild lilac trees, raspberry bushes, and violets. After crossing the Satchou, we do not meet nearly so many people suffering from goitre as we had done in the villages further west, and the population seems to be altogether more vigorous and cheerful, having been put in better heart than usual this year by the frequency of the rains. Some ill-natured people had announced our coming, and had added that we should bring a drought with us. But as we brought rain instead, our partisans were triumphant, and we received a very friendly greeting.

May 15.—We left the banks of the river this morning, and penetrated into the pine forests of the mountain-side, our bivouac being in a glade near a torrent. The rain is falling in heavy showers, but the natives whom we employ to collect wood for the fires are young and cheerful, and go to work with a light heart, cracking their jokes as unconcernedly as if it were quite dry overhead and underfoot.

From the time of crossing the Satchou we meet with several instances of an admixture of Mongolian blood, of which we had seen very few cases previously. The people, who have broader faces, are not rich, but their country abounds with game, and we add several animal specimens to our collection.

May 17.—We have scaled a pass of nearly 15,000 feet, passing bare rocks covered with snow, and assailed by a snow-storm, which reminds us that winter is not yet over. Descending to Routéoundo we see a lot of monkeys, two of which we kill; while Rachmed captures a new-born one, which he puts under the care of the little she-ape we have had with us since we left Houmda, where we bought her from some Chinese soldiers.* She takes so much care of her bantling that she suffocates it, and it is a touching spectacle to see her licking the little body and trying to recall it to life.

In this region the tribes are somewhat independent, and as

* She is now in the Jardin des Plantes, Paris—*Translator.*

BRIDGE AT SOUGOMBA.

it sometimes happens that several different tribes supply a contingent of porters and carriers, there are frequent quarrels as to the distribution of loads, these quarrels not ceasing until one of the chiefs draws lots.

May 19.—Traversing grassy steppes, where the bears go about in large groups, descending into gorges, and scaling some bare plateaus, we to-day reached Koushoune, and again saw men armed with swords and carrying rifles. They are taller than any we have seen before, and have regular features and a proud air, looking at us with a certain amount of contempt. They made a difficulty about supplying us with yaks, and when these animals had been brought, the chiefs discussed angrily amongst themselves whether we should be allowed to load them. Permission being given at last, we crossed the Latchou, near a village where a Chinaman carries on trade. After a three hours' march the drivers refused to advance further, and began unloading their animals, with the intention of leaving us in the desert. We had to take prompt action, and compelled them to advance by flourishing a revolver over their heads, but they did so at a very slow rate, and with a sneering sort of laugh, pretending that they must stop again to load the yaks better. However, we made them understand that this was no time for joking, and forced them to step along for five hours, but had to look so closely after them that there was no time to go after the bears to be seen all about the steppe. Rachmed killed one yesterday.

In the evening we make friends with our yak-drivers, and they promise to do a long stage the next day. It freezes at night, for we are at 8,450 feet, the minimum being 25°.

May 20.—Having found some warm springs not far from our camp, we descended the valley as far as Ouoshishoune, where we saw black tents on the river-banks. The chief of the district came to say that two Chinamen had brought him orders not to sell us anything, but he did not intend to obey them, and would let us have as many yaks and horses as we might require. This is a simple matter, for stock of all kinds is abundant, and a good sheep is to be had for a rupee.

We are visited by several lamas, one of them being an enormous man, and this strikes us all the more because we have seen so many thin people since we entered Thibet. Fatness is the appanage of the chiefs and of the rich in this, as in all other Eastern countries; and it is curious to note that the same Thibetan word (*bembo*) is used to designate high rank, or the good condition of a sheep or yak, just as *gordo*, in Spanish, is alike applied to fat or to wealthy people. While upon questions of philology, I may mention that the cuckoo, which has received an onomatopœian name in all languages, is *kouti* in Thibetan, *kounjou* in Chinese, *kakouska* in Russian, *kakou* in the Tarantshi dialect, and *pakou* in Uzbeg.

To return to the lamas, those at Ouoshishoune lead a very easy life. Here, too, we are eye-witnesses of a procession, in which a lama rides a horse led by two women, who are preceded by four others burning sweet herbs, the incense of which rises up to his nostrils, while six more bear presents that have been given him for the prayers he has recited. The good man rides imperturbably on, grinding his prayer-mill.

May 21.—To-day we meet with another lama on horseback, protected from the sun by a peaked straw hat with broad brim, and followed by three women, bare-footed and bare-headed, driving three yaks which were carrying his luggage.

May 22.—We reach Dzérine by way of mountains which might rather be called hills, and as no more snowy peaks are to be seen on the horizon, it might be imagined that we were about to emerge upon the plain. But this is only due to the cramped horizon, for as soon as we scale a pass we see by what a chaos of peaks, ridges, and chains we are shut in; indeed, we shall see nothing more of the plain until we reach the Tonquin delta.

CROSSING THE SATCHOU.

At Dzérine we receive a visit from the second Thibetan chief of the Goundjo, who tells us that the Chinese are doing all they can to prevent us from going to Batang, that they have vehemently urged his superior to refuse us the means of transport and provisions, but that the latter would do as we desired. Having arranged for him to accompany us until we have found an interpreter speaking both Thibetan and Chinese, as he does, we make arrangements for the transport of our baggage; and as the population of Dzérine is not large enough to supply all the porters we require, the chief sends out horsemen and men on foot to requisition them. The porters arrive in due course, many of them being very tall, and measuring six feet two inches. They have very large faces, with the skull tapering to a point, like an egg, dental prognathism being the general rule. They are very vigorous and good-natured, playing together like children; their houses are built like those we saw at preceding stages, though here and there are attempts at windows with wooden shutters.

May 24.—Leaving Dzérine with a caravan composed of several petty chiefs, who are most anxious to serve us, we followed the narrow valley until we reached, by an adjacent gorge, above which is built a lama-house, a gentle ascent leading to a pass of 13,100 feet, after having crossed a first one at an altitude of 150 feet less. This stage was got through very cheerily, our carriers singing and amusing themselves all the way, like packs of schoolboys, and greeting us with a smile every time they passed us.

By way of wooded plateaus and mountain spurs, where bears, wolves, foxes, and pheasants abound, we reached a gorge leading to the village of Hassar, which is perched upon a promontory at the junction of the gorge with the valley where flows the river Maktchou. There are a few patches of marsh and of cultivated land in the delta, and we watch the ploughs, drawn by yaks, at work, followed by men sowing the grain, who walk along with measured tread, while the women stand about and call out to frighten away the crows and pigeons, which fly off to the willow trees lining the pathway. The slopes of the mountain are bare of trees, and it is only very high up that one can see any pines overhanging the heights where the flocks are feeding.

The houses of Hassar are all crowded together on two sides of a street. It is not every day that one sees a street in Thibet, but we lose no time in going off to encamp on a piece of fallow. The curiosity our presence excites is good-natured, and the chiefs endeavour to meet our wishes, as we have gained a reputation for being generous, and it is known that we give medicine to those who ask for it, but that, while paying handsomely for what is done for us, we will not stand any nonsense. Our lama, Losène, is very useful to us, as he has the art of being at once patient and energetic, while he frightens the recalcitrants by warning them that we are terrible people owing to our arms of precision. Now and then we awe the natives by the distance we fire a bullet, and by the number of birds we kill at one shot. Losène, to whom we have repeated the thing a score of times, represents us as being "very good to those who are good, and very hard upon the bad."

Not far from our tent is a naked boy, three or four years of age, who has an enormous head, a big stomach, and a bent spine. The poor child cannot walk, his legs having no power, and one can tell by his deformed knees and hands that he is in the habit of dragging himself along like some creeping thing. He has a bestial expression, and a dull, lifeless eye. The chief of the district helps him up, to show us that he cannot stand without support, and exclaims, "No father or mother."

Our lama Losène takes a piece of money out of his purse and gives it to the poor boy. This kindness of heart differentiates the Thibetans from the Chinese, for again and again have I seen people dying of hunger in the Celestial Empire without anyone paying the slightest heed to them; while the ferocity and evil disposition of Chinese children is something incredible.

In the valley of the Maktchou were many houses in ruins, and the natives, being questioned as to who demolished them, replied that this was the work of the Sokpou, who live in the north, and that the latter, having heard that the lama-houses to the south contained a good deal of treasure, made a raid upon the district, massacring the inhabitants and burning the houses and forests.

In reply to further questions on the same subject, we were told that the survivors of these massacres returned and asked for assistance from the neighbouring tribes. Money was found for them by the lamas, and the fortresses and crenelated walls on the hills were built. They had been allowed to fall into disrepair since a sense of security returned, no recent attacks having been made by these Sokpou.

"But can you explain more precisely where these Sokpou live?"

"They live on the route taken by the servants whom you sent back before we started on our journey. Their country is further off than Natchou."

"In the Tsaïdam, then?"

"Yes, that's it."

"And when did this invasion take place?"

"A very long time ago."

This is one more proof of how impossible it is in the East to obtain the slightest historical information. It would seem as if the present alone interested them. Trustworthy documents are not to be had, and the historians who are content to derive their materials from Asiatic sources are not likely to understand much of the past which they seek to revive.

May 27.—Leaving Hassar, we mounted the course of a river

which winds about among lofty rocks, forming a narrow defile. A very awkward pathway, a rough sort of staircase cut in the rocks, leads to a cultivated valley three or four miles long, where inhabited villages and numerous ruins are to be seen. Once more taking the south-easterly direction which we had abandoned for a time, we climbed a plateau and descended again into another valley, where we came upon the village of Akker. Our arrival was heralded by thunder and lightning, and we took refuge from the storm under some fine poplars, when we had time to note that the fields were well cultivated and enclosed, and that value is placed upon timber, some small poplars recently planted having been surrounded by thorns to prevent the cattle from getting at them. When the sun came out after the rain, the valley seemed to be a sea of blood, for the soil is quite red, and glittered after being so deluged with rain.

Having changed our beasts of burden at Akker, we pitched our camp at Lendjoune, on a small plateau with just room for a score of houses. Our tent is near a spring, under poplars which at a distance we took for willows owing to the similarity of foliage.

The inhabitants, having seen that we shot the small birds, try to frighten them away by throwing stones. They appear the most insolent of the people we have met with so far. The native chiefs exercise an administrative rather than a patriarchal authority. Thus the Thibetan chief who accompanies us has a copper cup out of which he is in the habit of drinking, and this cup, which he has left for a moment, suddenly disappears. No one has seen it, of course, but when he tells two of his men to seize one of the onlookers and flog him till the cup is returned, it reappears as if by magic.

In the evening, when the flocks are being driven home, we hear a doleful dirge like that of the Mussulman women who accompany the dead to the cemetery, and very possibly a body is being taken up to be laid out on the summit of the mountain.

At night, when we leave for Dotou, there is a fall of rain, with a cloudy sky and north wind.

May 28.—We are told that two Chinese from Ba and one from Tsiamdo are awaiting us at Dotou. The Chinese mandarin recently sent from Pekin to Lhassa has just been through Ba and Tsiamdo, and we are informed that, having been apprised of our journey by the Thibetan authorities, he told them they were to assist us, and that his predecessor said the same. Be this as it may, the Thibetans will help us in carrying our luggage as far as Tatsien-Lou, and it is the reverse of unpleasant to have these promises renewed just as we are about to come into contact with the Chinese authorities.

The ride to Dotou from Lendjoune is over some bare table-lands, and a very easy pass of 10,800 feet, leading to a region undulating like the last spurs of a mountain chain. A few hamlets are to be seen in the low ground, a few ruins on the hills, and the whitened walls of a few lama-houses, but there are no more wooden houses, this not being a forest region. In three hours' time we arrive at the lama-house of Dotou, built upon a level piece of ground near the Maktchou river, and are soon surrounded by a crowd of inquisitive people, who hold their noses, either out of disgust or astonishment.

A few paces from where our tent is pitched is another inhabited by the Chinese of whom mention was made to us at Lendjoune. These latter mix for a few minutes with the crowd which is having a look at us, and then return to their tent, emerging from it soon after in state to pay us a visit. Their chief is a petty mandarin with a white button, equivalent to about the rank of corporal, but that does not prevent him from addressing us with great dignity. Having shown his card and greeted us by pressing his fists close together, he says he has been sent by the chief of Djankalo (Changka) in order to welcome us and accompany us further on. He is entirely at our disposal, and hopes we will come to his tent and take a cup of tea. In fact, he had been beginning to get uneasy about us, as

GROUP OF NATIVES.

he had expected us a week sooner, and was afraid that some accident had happened. However, he was very glad we had arrived safely, as his provisions were beginning to run short, but now he could send off a messenger to his superior at Changka and say that we had arrived all right. After this avalanche of

SCENE IN INHABITED TRIBET.

compliments, he withdrew with comic gravity. I may add that there are no people who possess the art of assimilation to so perfect a degree as the Chinese, who can either ascend or descend the social ladder with astonishing rapidity.

The principal attraction of the Dotou lama-house is a series of prayer-mills. Beneath a gallery running almost entirely round the house, are enormous bobbins composed of printed prayers and transfixed by a long piece of wood which is held in position by two beams. These bobbins are turned by hand, and as it is said that each is composed of 10,000 prayers, and as there are at least 100 of them, it is easy to see what an enormous quantity of prayers can be said in a walk round the building. Our arrival, however, distracted the worshippers from their pious occupation, and when we unloaded our beasts, they came and felt the weight of our packages and wanted to put their hands on our clothes, their attitude being intolerably insolent. What interested them most was our wild-yak skin, which they would have pulled all to pieces if we had not made them keep their hands off it.

I had scarcely gone into my tent when Prince Henry called me to come out, and when I went I found a free fight going on, with Rachmed holding down a man all covered with blood, and others flourishing their swords or throwing stones. Akoun and Abdullah effected a clearance by firing a few shots from their revolvers in the air, and the Chinese made off, leaving two or three of their comrades prisoners, including the man on whose chest Rachmed had got his knee. The cause of the disturbance, as it then appeared, was that this latter, one of the chiefs, had tried to handle the yak-skin, in spite of Rachmed's injunction, and so from words they had come to blows. However, in response to the entreaties of our lama, we set the captives at liberty again, and then our Chinese friends, who had held well aloof while all this was going on, appeared on the scene, and, assuming the most valiant air, went out on the terrace of the lama-house, overlooking the place whither our assailants had fled. The chief then came back, and in the course of a conversation said these people were quite beyond management. "We give them good advice," he added, "but it is all to no purpose. They are such ill-conducted savages that neither at Pekin nor Lhassa is it thought desirable to have them for subjects. It is quite impossible to quit the high road and penetrate into their mountain retreats, and we never meet them without there being disputes. Last year they robbed an envoy of the Emperor, and they recently refused to provide beasts of burden for our mandarin who was going to Lhassa. We ourselves could only get these horses by holding out threats that you would fire on them when you came. Nothing is to be done with them by reasoning; and if we use force they give us back blow for blow. So all we can do is to leave them alone, though we have 1,300 men distributed over the posts between Lhassa and Tatsien-Lou."

When we looked at the three soldiers whom the Liantaï (treasurer-payer) of Batang had sent us as a protection, we could not help smiling to one another. It is easy to understand that the Thibetans do not feel any alarm when they see them coming.

These three men do not convey a very high idea of the Chinese army, for one is a bloodless opium-smoker, devoid of all vigour, shivering in the mountain air, though we are barely 10,000 feet high, so sensitive to cold that he covers up his ears even in the daytime, as well as his head and neck. He has yellow teeth and a lack-lustre eye, and it is as much as he can do to keep on his horse. He admits that his pay is six rupees a month, and that he spends half of it on tobacco. As to the wearer of the white button, whom we have nicknamed the "Colonel," he does not smoke opium, and is a most consequential little man. It is amusing to see him strut about, swinging his arms, straddling his legs and bending his figure, while his hands with their long finger-nails are, with much assumption, thrust out of his broad sleeves.

The third is not so martial or warlike, and has been sent to join the two others because he speaks Thibetan. Unlike theirs, his nose is not *retroussé*, his features being regular.

At Dotou we dismissed our guide, the lama Losène, who was delighted with the presents we gave him, including a few chromos representing lion-shooting in Algeria, and bear-hunting in the Ural. He bade us farewell with emotion, and wished us a pleasant journey. Although we have a Thibetan interpreter, and, after leaving Changka, shall meet Chinese military posts, the worthy Losène urged us to be on our guard, for, as far as Batang, we should traverse a region inhabited by very ill-disposed and dangerous men, who might attack us as we went through the mountains.

May 29.—Bearing this in mind, we take our cartridges and keep close to our baggage, with an eye on the ridges above. The route we follow reminds us of the highlands of Thibet, and we see many flocks under the watchful eye of shepherds, who carry long guns with forked rests at the end of them, and live in black tents which are protected by their fierce dogs. All trace of vegetation has disappeared, whereas a few days ago we could have fancied ourselves in the Alps, with jasmine, lilac, tulips, and poppies all about us. Sleet is falling, with a bitterly cold southeast wind, and we wonder if winter is going to return.

Leaving the valley which we have followed since Dotou, we traversed a pass of over 13,000 feet leading to an undulating steppe, with peat-bogs and a few black tents, dotted about with flocks. We halted near these tents, the occupants of which were not so rudely inquisitive as the natives of Dotou, and learnt that the place is called Gato by the Chinese and Hado by the Thibetans. The route from Hado to Tara first lies over a pass of 13,000 feet, and then through a grassy valley, beyond which are some pine-clad slopes, with a few patches of cultivated land within half an hour of Tara. There are no traces of irrigation, but beyond Tara, which is situated upon a sort of natural terrace, vegetation reappears, the pines, the poplars, the oak with leaves like those of the holly-tree, the wild raspberry, and the thorn, giving the valley a delicious odour. Where the valley opens out, a chapel has been built, and above is a lama-house. Following the right bank of the Tson-ron, we passed through various hamlets. As wood is plentiful, there are a great many chapels and *châlets* built of the material, so that we might again fancy ourselves on the Alps. The inhabitants are a fine set of men, some of whom wear hats with broad white brims, and look like the Mexican Gauchos, while their wives have so far modified their dress that they wear petticoats tightened at the waist, instead of tying their pelisses tight over their haunches.

The whole of this valley is full of animation, and in the pinewoods to the south of it, the villages are perched like nests among the verdure. We halted at Tsonké, the houses of which are built upon the left bank of an affluent of the Tson-ron, with a white walled lama-house on an eminence above. The chiefs of this village were very civil, and were ready to supply us with what we wanted. Their horses, however, are not what they might be, though bigger than those we had hitherto had, this increase in size being due, as we were told, to their having been crossed with the Sininfou breed.

May 30.—The stage from Tsonké to Tchounneu is a delightful one, for on leaving the valley the road rises at once to a plateau covered with pines and oaks—the leaves of which are like those of holly—and dotted here and there with grassy glades and with gorges in which torrents babble. The path is through the wood, well protected from the sun, and with squirrels darting from branch to branch. By way of two small passes we got to Tchounneu, and encamped in an enclosed meadow, a mild south-east wind making things very agreeable. The inhabitants appear to be rather violent, judging by the readiness with which one of them drew his sword when one of our men told him to keep his hands off our luggage. The incident, however, was not repeated.

The Thibetan interpreter chatted part of the evening with us, and said that, as we had assumed from his regular features, his father was a Mussulman, and that he was quite young when he came to Batang with the missionary Lou.* He described this missionary as being very kind and intelligent, speaking and writing both Chinese and Thibetan very correctly, as giving all he had to the poor, and as knowing all about everything, even the mending of a watch.

Europeans may smile at the idea of a man being regarded as wonderful because he knows how to set a watch right, but the Chinese only recognise our superiority to them in the art of constructing machinery, if they do even in that. To return to our interpreter, who is a Christian, though he does not like to own to it, he is the father of five children, and he has been selected to come and meet us because he speaks Thibetan and Chinese. Asked as to why he had left Father Lou, he said, "I did not leave him. He died twenty years ago, without a priest by his bedside, surrounded by his Christians, who adored him, and who were heart-broken. Before death, he said where he would like to be buried, indicating a spot on the mountain-side, where he had planted a small knife in the ground. We did as he bade us, and when we get to Changka, I will show you the place."

"Have you remained at Changka since?"

"No, I went to Batang."

"Why did you not stay there?"

"Then you don't know that the Christians were driven out from there two years ago, the lower classes having been excited against them?"

"By whom?"

"By some ill-disposed persons who accused them of having been the cause of the drying-up of a lake in the mountain, which admits of the fields about Batang being irrigated. So the people

* Father Renou, as I afterwards discovered.

destroyed the houses and chapel of the Christians, and drove them away, the school-teacher, who attempted to protect the holy books, being killed."

"What did the Chinese mandarin say?"

"Nothing."

"Were no damages paid for this?"

"It appears that the missionaries will get some, for you have a Minister at Pekin, who has put in a claim to the Tsong-li-Yamen, and we are told that justice will be done. In the meanwhile, we have to dissimulate, and many Christians have died of starvation."

"You acknowledge you are Christians. Why did you not say so sooner?"

"I had seen that there was a priest among you, and I even thought the chief was a bishop in disguise, for we are expecting fresh priests."

Thus it was that we heard about the destruction of the Batang Mission, which Monsignor Biet, Bishop of Tatsien-Lou, had already announced by a letter in the *Missions catholiques;* and at the same time we learnt that the Chinese Government readily makes fine promises which it does not keep, and that foreign diplomatists are easily contented with smooth words, wrongly imagining that the interests of Europe can be separated from those of the Catholic missionaries. If they were to travel in the heart of the Celestial Empire, they would see that a European is considered by the people as the representative of a nation which is loathed, and which, though tolerated on the coast, is maltreated and killed at every available opportunity inland. To submit to the pillage of the missions, is to encourage attacks upon the Consulates.

June 1.—When we resume our journey, the weather is delightful, the minimum for the night having been 65°, while the fact of its being the 1st of June, and of our being due in a month at Tatsien-Lou, where we shall get news of Europe, imparts fresh vigour to our steps as we descend the valley. We only hope that the meeting with the mandarins at Changka and Batang may not raise fresh difficulties to delay our first

RUINS IN THE KTCHOU VALLEY (p. 165).

meeting with Europeans, a few days hence. The valley is pleasant enough, with its fields of scanty barley, and its stream with salt deposit on the banks; and as we get a little further on, we come upon a lama-house built upon a promontory at the junction of two valleys. All the lamas are out on the walls to see us pass, and most of them are remarkable for their corpulence.

From the valley we climb to a tableland covered with pine woods, and reach the pass of 18,000 feet which leads down to Changka. Westward appears another valley, from which emerge long files of yaks carrying heavy loads, and our interpreter says it is the high road to Lhassa, while, pointing to two upright stones, he tells us that it is at the foot of them that Father Lou and another Christian are buried. It is rather strange that a French tomb should be found at the meeting-place of the ways

LAMA-HOUSE AT DOTOU (p. 170).

which other Frenchmen have been the first to trace in the unknown land of Thibet, for at Changka we shall get on to the route of Fathers Huc and Gabet, which, at a later period, Fathers Renou, Fage, and Desgodins followed for some distance.

A Chinaman arrives on foot, and says that the mandarin of Changka wishes to receive us in state, and as a few green trees, surrounded by a palisade, are visible in the small plain, we express a desire to encamp beneath their shade. We are agreeably surprised to find that this has already been done, our tastes having already been made known in advance by the mandarin who had gone on in front. So we make our way towards the town of Changka, if the name of town can be given to a small group of houses; and as we enter, we find the garrison of the place drawn up in line. It consists of about twenty warriors of all ages, whose sole weapon is an oilskin parasol. They have all of them a most woebegone and starved appearance, and, as may be seen from their glassy look and emaciated features, most of them are opium-smokers. In order to conform with Chinese etiquette, we alight from our horses and pass in front of these troops, who do us honour by kneeling on the ground and pronouncing words which we do not comprehend. Then we mount our horses again and go off to the garden, which is shut in by tall and leafy poplars. The crowd, composed of Thibetans, Chinese, and half-breeds, surges round us with noisy and disdainful curiosity, and escorts us to the tents which the mandarin has had put up for us.

Very soon after our arrival we receive a visit from four soldiers, one of whom has accompanied us from Dotou, and from two white buttons, including the corporal whose consequential appearance is described above. They have come to present the respects of the garrison, and to offer us a box of *zamba* and a box of beans, in which one or two dozen eggs have been placed; but while they are making their genuflections, their attendants whip off the boxes—for fear, no doubt, that we shall accept the presents. This is a great disappointment to Abdullah, who dotes on eggs, and so it is to Rachmed and Akoun, who load the garrison with insults, and only recover their equanimity when they see five other warriors arrive with a table in the form of a large wicker basket, which they are carrying on their shoulders with a pole, and inside which are visible several cups filled with different ingredients. This, the corporal informs us, is a repast sent by the mandarin of Changka, who regrets that he is not well enough to pay us a visit to-day, but hopes to do so to-morrow. After thanking him for his kind attention, we ask the speaker to supply us with some fresh eggs, chicken, and pork—for we have seen several pigs about the streets. The corporal promises to go and see about this, and we sit down to table, in the literal sense of the word, for the first time these many months past. The staple of the meal consists of slices of pork and chicken cut up into small pieces. The whole is cooked in pig's lard, and Rachmed makes off, like the good Mussulman he is, while Abdullah, whose voracity is stronger than all the prescriptions of the Koran, enjoys the rather tasteless dishes, followed by a dessert of balls of pastry—inside which are bits of coloured sugar —and a small bottle of *ara*—a horrible concoction of spirit.

This meal delights several of our men who have got tired of the bad food on the road, mutton and goat flesh being so repugnant to some of them that they can only eat bread, or rather a paste made of barley or bean meal. While we are enjoying this repast, a Thibetan chief, who is the most important man in the region, arrives, and treats us with great civility. It seems that orders were sent to Changka concerning us three weeks ago by the Chinese chief at Lhassa, and that six weeks ago it was known that twelve men with camels were advancing on Lhassa; the Ta-Lama of which had sent orders about us to the lamas and the Thibetan people.

When we ask to whom the garden where we are encamped belongs, we are told it is the property of the garrison, and when we inquire how this is, the answer was, " It used to belong to Chinese bonzes, who had built a pagoda surrounded by trees, but the Thibetans, having risen in rebellion, killed the bonzes and destroyed the pagoda. Then the Chinese collected numerous troops, again reduced the Thibetans to subjection, and, in order to punish the rebels, insisted, among other things, that this ground should be made over to the garrison of Changka. The soldiers have put a wall round it, and feed their stock there, while, as the site is a convenient one, it has been used for entertainments, promenades, religious festivals, and military parades."

"Do the soldiers often drill?"

"Now and then."

"When did they drill last?"

"Two years ago."

"Why don't they drill oftener?"

"They have no arms. There are only four swords at Changka for 150 men; the others are in the stores at Batang."

"Are there really 150 soldiers? We have not seen more than thirty or so since we came."

"There ought to be, for the mandarin draws pay for that number. But as he himself receives a salary of not more than five or six ounces of silver a month, he increases his pay by reducing the contingent. Those who die are not replaced, and as most of the soldiers are married, their male children are put down on the roll, so that they may receive their father's pay when they are old enough to take their place. This is why you have seen lads of thirteen or fourteen among the soldiers drawn up in line to salute you."

"Which are the unmarried soldiers?"

"The opium smokers, who have not enough money left to keep a wife and family."

"The women are Thibetans, are they not?"

"Thibetans or half-breeds."

When the corporal has gone, the old interpreter confides to us that he will not come with us to Batang, for, he says, "Our chief hates me, and I know that he is intriguing with the mandarin to accompany you farther, and as the mandarin is, like him, a native of Setchou, he is sure to have his way and take my place." We ask the interpreter to get in a good supply of eggs, for we have not much confidence in the corporal, and we know how readily the Chinese promise all one asks, and how cleverly they get out of keeping their word. Still, we have been told that we shall have some fresh pork to-morrow, and we go to bed dreaming of broiled chops, which are sure to be delicious.

PRAYER-MILL AT DOTOU (p. 170).

CHAPTER XV.

BATANG, TATSIEN-LOU, AND TONQUIN.

Religious Prophylactics—"Red" and "Yellow" Lamaism—The Lamas as Capitalists—From Changka to Kouskou—The Tea Trade between China and Thibet—Leindünne—Anarchy—Chinese Inns—The Blue River (Kin-sha-Kiang)—Frenchmen in Thibet—Chinese Justice—An Orgie—Chinese Soldiers: the Courage of Numbers—At Batang—A Series of Questions—Tatsien-Lou—The French Missionaries there—A Difficulty with the Mandarin—Apology—Chinese Administration—Sending Home the Photographs—The Red River—On French Soil—Hanoï—The Future of Tonquin—Conclusion.

A DANCER.

June 2.—Last night there was a minimum temperature of 27°, and there has been a south wind all the morning, followed by rain. Three shots announced that this was the fifteenth day of the Chinese month, when the people go to the pagoda to do reverence to the statues, the secretary of the mandarin informing us that his master had gone there, and might be too occupied all the rest of the day to pay us his promised visit, while he would not like to intrude upon us in the evening.

Then he handed us a long letter in Chinese and Thibetan, which, upon his reading it out, told us that, having arrived on the fourteenth day of the moon, we were to leave on the sixteenth, and that we were to be provided with six saddle-horses, six pack-horses, and thirty-three yaks. Two soldiers were to go ahead and collect the horses, while two others were to accompany us. And in five days we were to reach Batang. This piece of news was very welcome, for we had had enough of arguing and contending at each relay. So we thanked the representative of the authorities, and asked him to convey our compliments to the mandarin, just making an allusion to the promised fresh pork. He said that some should be sent to us forthwith, but Chinese superstitions, concerning which I might, if time allowed, write a long chapter, prevented us from eating the flesh of one of the small black pigs which run about in Changka. The lamas had ordered the slaughter-house of the town to be closed, because prayers were at this moment being offered up for rain, and it would not do to offend the deity by an act of bloodshed. To kill a pig at this moment would excite the anger of the gods, and the harvest would be endangered. So it was all up with the pork chops.

The whole population is given over to prayer, men, women, and children pouring out to the white tents pitched in the plain, where the lamas have conveyed the statues of their gods, and are making supplications to them. It is not at all unlikely that our presence is the cause of these religious prophylactics, for fear that we may have cast a spell upon the ground we have trodden. A short time ago, we saw the Thibetans pass our baggage over the fire so as to purify it before they put it on their shoulders, while on another occasion the men who were at work in the fields we went through, snatched up a handful of earth—like Marius predicting the birth of the Gracchi—and, throwing it into the air, mumbled a form of prayer to disinfect the soil.

All the devout people of Changka are astir and on their way to the tents, and a horse is led carrying six packets of very long prayers pressed tight between slabs of wood and fastened with strips of leather. Then comes a fat lama of high rank, riding at his ease upon a mule led by two lamas bareheaded, who hold the reins in one hand, while with the other they turn their prayer-mills. Behind them come the bearers of drums and cymbals, and last of all a crowd of clerical and lay worshippers, marching cheerfully along. All the lamas of Changka and their flocks have turned out to avert the misfortune which our presence is calculated to bring upon the valley. It appears that the divinity had been entreated for some little time past to send rain, and that these prayers were just about being answered when we arrived. As strangers could not be other than hostile, the lamas had no difficulty in persuading the faithful that the clouds would disperse without sending down any rain unless they were kept back by fervent prayers. So the lamas of Changka are said to be unfavourably disposed towards us, the more so as they are "reds," that is to say, they have not accepted the Tsongkapa reform, the partizans of which are distinguished by their yellow head-gear. These "reds" were much annoyed at the receipt of the letters from Lhassa, commending us to their favour, for the theocracy of Lhassa is "yellow," and the lamas of the old school say that we shall be the cause of terrible drought; and they will not lend any aid in the transporting of our luggage. They also decline to lend us any yaks, so that the chiefs of the neighbouring tribes have to do all the work.

A certain antagonism always reigns between the lay and the religious chiefs. But the latter are the richer and more influential.

The lama-house of Changka owns a good part of the valley, and in course of time it will be in possession of the whole, the lamas being the only people who have any capital in hand, so that they lend money to the poor, and enrich themselves by usury. A time arrives when the debtors are unable to pay, and then they surrender their land and become in reality serfs attached to the glebe. From that time they become themselves the property of the lama-house, which furnishes them with implements, seed, and manure to cultivate the soil, and they make over the harvest to their new masters, being paid in flour—enough to keep them from starvation during the winter.

These red lamas are not all given up to celibacy or to a life devoid of worldly pleasures, for, when tired of the cloister, they are at liberty to resume a lay life, on condition of abandoning to the community the endowment they paid for admission. In the same way, if, once more tired of ordinary life, they knock a second time at the door of the monastery, they are re-admitted if prepared to make a second payment. Whenever

DANCERS AT CHANGKA.

a property is for sale, these lamas buy it. When, therefore, they pray for rain, they are really praying for themselves. In this instance it is to be supposed that their prayers are answered, or else that we are not such very dreadful people, for there is a fall of snow and rain during the night. This ought to put the lamas and their serfs in a good humour, but the former are most splenetic, and continue to look at us askance. One of them distinguishes himself by the persistency with which he drives off the inquisitive people who come to look at us. He is a long, thin sort of fellow, emaciated, no doubt, by constant privations; with his long eagle-like nose, his hollow cheeks, and his sharp chin with its tuft of hair, he has anything but a taking appearance. From time to time he makes a dash into our enclosure, scolds the inquisitive people who have collected, and drives them off to the door, raising his arms as a shepherd does when driving a flock of sheep. He, at all events, seems to be a thorough-paced bachelor, judging by the unceremonious way in which he treats the women.

June 16.—The rain comes down in torrents, but that does not damp the ardour with which these lamas turn their prayer-mills as they march behind us, as if they wished to purify the soil we have been treading. The people, however, escort us a little way, and the Changka garrison, thanking us for our presents, wishes us a pleasant journey. As we descend the valley, which gradually narrows, we meet numerous caravans of yaks conveying tea, and at Poula we obtain a relay after a march of sixty lis, or a little over eleven miles, which would show that the measure of the li is not definitely settled, or that the Chinese have, for some reason, exaggerated the length of the stage. Thinking eleven miles a very short journey for people in so much of a hurry, we do not allow ourselves to be tempted by the meal of pork, fish, and *peshké* (a kind of cabbage) which is served us in a white tent, and insist upon pushing on to Koushou, as had been arranged before the start. But it seems as if there was no intention of keeping faith with us, and, after some discussion, the chief of the lamas and the civil chief of the district arrive. They tell us that we cannot start till to-morrow, and that we must await the return of the yaks, which have gone on to Changka with bales of tea.

We ask if these persons have received orders, and the mandarin's men declare that either last night or early this morning they were advised of our arrival and told to keep yaks for our use. As we are in possession of an enormous sealed document, authorising us to requisition beasts of burden in the name of the Emperor of China, we protest, and request the white-buttoned mandarin, who has escorted us from Dotou to Changka, to speak on our behalf, telling him that he was a powerful chief and that the Thibetans would obey him at once. But he says they are not under his jurisdiction, and goes on smoking his pipe in an unconcerned sort of way. So we take the matter into our own hands, and by dint of parleying, discussing, threatening, and promising, get what we want, and go to pass the night at Koushou, a military post in the hollow of a small valley. The road to it is through woods and over a pass 12,400 feet high, whence we can distinguish to the west a white chain which the natives call Dameloune, so far as we can understand them. While eating a good-sized omelette with bacon, about

A BUDDHIST CHAPEL.

10 p.m., we learn from the commander of this fort that in two days' time we shall be on the territory of Batang, and that our arrival has been looked forward to very eagerly.

June 17.—The road we follow is that of the pilgrims, and it is marked by numerous *obos* with large quantities of engraved prayers. We also notice on the *obos*, and on the top of the chapels, small columns of wood, surmounted by balls, by crescents, or other roughly-carved ornaments, but all done in exactly the same way. Each of these columns has twelve hollow rings, and this figure twelve, which is constantly recurring, must tally with some religious or superstitious fancy. We asked explanations as to this from competent persons, but were unable to get any. I can only guess, therefore, that it has something to do with the Thibetan cycle of twelve years.

Certain authors have stated that Lhassa is the resort of countless pilgrims. I do not know upon what they base their statements, but we met very few, and there must be some mistake, unless, indeed, the population in the south of Thibet and to the north of the Himalayas is very dense, and so devout that it supplies the great bulk of the pilgrims.

The tea trade between China and Thibet is very important, the transport being effected chiefly by the road from Tatsien-Lou to Lhassa, by way of Tsiamdo. The relays of yaks are settled by custom, each village contributing its share to the conveyance of the tea, and receiving a fixed contribution, generally in kind.

Three hours after leaving Koushou we get a relay at Leindünne, where we arrive by way of cultivated valleys and plantations of oak and pine, the people appearing to be better off in every way than those in the districts we have been passing through. Some of them are even fat, and the women are of a more civilised type—both as regards appearance and dress—than the Thibetans. Their clothes are of coarse cloth, sometimes red, sometimes striped in the Thibetan colours of green, red, and yellow. In the sunlight this blending of colours produces a very striking effect, reminding one of Andalusia.

Beyond Leindünne the route branches off to Batang in one direction and to Atentze in another, the journey to the latter place occupying, according to the Chinese soldiers, four days; while from Atentze to Yunnan-Fou it would take a month. But the road is so bad that it can only be done on foot. The best account of this region is to be found in the work of the French missionaries Desgodins and Biet.

Although the valleys are well cultivated, the crops are not sufficient to feed the military post at Leindünne, which is obliged to get its supplies from Atentze; and although the post

THE KIN-SHA-KIANG (GREAT BLUE RIVER) (p. 195).

is within a two days' march of Batang, nothing is bought there, prices being too high. While we are gossiping we see some splendid mules, richly caparisoned, and carrying bales of tea, being driven by; they belong, we are told, to the Talai-Lama in person, who sends them round with tea every year to the different lama-houses. The houses in this village present some attempt at decoration, in the shape of corbels and patterns on the window-shutters; while, to judge by the large quantity of *manis* (engraved prayers) freshly painted in bright colours, this must be a land of holiness. We cannot, however, ascertain whether the peasants, in picking up a handful of soil and throwing it into the air as we pass, are actuated by a religious motive or by the fear that we may bring them ill-luck.

June 18.—During the night there was snow and rain; and as the rain is still falling at dawn, our Chinese soldiers give us another proof of their reluctance to travel in the wet. These men are quite useless, their authority over the Thibetans being *nil;* and all they can do is to smoke their pipes and say "Io, Io." The whole country appears to be in a state of anarchy, and the native chiefs are not obeyed by their subjects.

It is eleven o'clock before we descend the valley with our baggage, and after an hour's march the animals are unloaded, and fresh disputes begin between men of different tribes.

While the natives are quarrelling over our baggage, we go to look at one of the water-mills at the edge of a stream. It is like all the mills in Asia, the water being supplied through the hollow trunk of a tree, with an undershot wheel setting the millstone in motion. In the centre of the upper stone is a hole, through which the grains drop into a bag made of goat-skin, held in its place by a rope tied to the wall.

After an hour and a half's talk the population consent to carry our baggage to the next relay, only two miles off; and from there, after fresh disputes, we arrive at Kountsetinne.

Having been driven out of the inn of the place—where we had intended passing the night—by its filthiness, we pitch our tent in the courtyard, bad as the weather is.

WOMEN AT BATANG.

I need not repeat my description of these filthy Chinese inns, which are so disgusting that those of Thibet seem palaces in comparison. It appears that this particular one is intended for the accommodation of the mandarins and soldiers on the march, and the keeper of it is very much disappointed at our leaving it, as he has been told that we pay liberally when we are well satisfied. However, we prefer to remain where we are, and while the Thibetan and Chinese chiefs are sitting quietly smoking their pipes and drinking their tea under cover from the rain, the two principal ones hurriedly mount their horses and gallop off with

LAMAS AT BATANG.

guns and swords. It appears that, a few hundred yards from the village, at the foot of the gorge, some brigands who had come down from the mountain have taken by surprise the Thibetans who were conveying our baggage, and seized six horses. In order to do this more easily, the brigands allowed the bulk of the escort to pass, and only attacked the rear-guard. Our "white button" says that it will be useless to pursue them, as they have got well away to the mountain; and when I ask him if this is a frequent occurrence, he says that it is, the mountain being peopled by incorrigible savages.

June 19.—There were heavy showers all night; and when we start this morning, the descent from the inn—which is at an altitude of about 8,000 feet—begins almost at once, and we are soon among clematis, syringas, jasmine, and eglantines, with cultivated fields, and nuts nearly ripe. Still descending, we find ripe barley at 5,400 feet; while about 1,000 feet below the people are gathering in the harvest. At 4,000 feet the harvest has already been got in, and we are able to give our horses fresh straw. The people inhabiting this slope of the mountain are rather fierce, and do not obey their chiefs better than those on the other side; but the dress is gradually being modified under the influence of Chinese fashions, and the native chiefs have the hair cropped close upon the front of the head, like the mandarins of the conquering nation. The people, too, do not wear the same sort of shoes as the Thibetans, the children having their feet in sandals, which are kept on by strips of leather passed between the toes and fastened round the heel.

As we follow a rather awkward path in the pouring rain, we suddenly come on a large river, in a valley nearly half a mile wide. This is the Kin-sha-Kiang, the great Blue River; but we cannot keep pace with its rapid current, for this river—the Yan-tse-kiang of the East—rolls its turbid flood at a tremendous pace over rocks and boulders, as if eager to bury its waters in the depths of the ocean. Leaving the river-bank again, we get upon a more easy route, and, galloping along past eglantine-trees, reach a delta formed by the Shisougoune as it emerges from the mountain. We cross it by a bridge which does not seem any too safe; and as we do so, we hear shots being fired from the high rocks on the other side. This is a salute from men who have been posted up there to keep a look-out for the brigands who infest the country, and they have received orders from the Chinese mandarin at Batang to look after us. A little farther on we pass a chapel built in the form of a triumphal arch, and thence descend to the banks of the Kin-sha-Kiang, the bed of which is so broad at this spot that it can be crossed in a large flat-bottomed boat 50 feet long by nearly 9 feet in beam. This boat, which is of deal secured with iron clamps, is rowed by two women and two men, all of mixed blood, with a long-tailed Chinaman steering. The river is about a furlong broad at the point where we cross it; and as we are being rowed across, we cannot but think of the Frenchmen who have done so before us, and who have scarcely had justice done them. Our countrymen are about the only people who have had the good fortune to visit Thibet since it has been closed against Europeans. First of all, there came Fathers Huc and Gabet, whose daring voyage will not have been forgotten, and who have been rather harshly criticised. They have been blamed for not having mentioned chains of mountains which the state of the atmosphere doubtless prevented them from seeing, and they have been laughed at for describing as a broad river what those who saw it thirty years afterwards found to be only a small one. But their critics seem to forget under what disadvantages they—the first Europeans to come into the country—laboured, and for my part I consider that they effected the most daring and interesting of journeys with little in the way of resources except their own will and energy.

Since leaving Changka we have been upon what may be described as French soil, for Father Renou penetrated into Thibet, and got together the materials for a dictionary which may be compared to that of Csoma, the learned Hungarian, whose labours he completed, thus opening the country to his successors by enabling them to study the language. Then came Fathers Fage, Desgodins, and Thomine, who penetrated as far as Tsiamdo, and many others whose names should be familiar to all Europeans. These martyrs of civilisation opened up the way for explorers, and the illustrious Prjevalsky, when travelling in Thibet, did no more than follow a portion of Father Huc's route; while the Englishmen, Gill and Mesny, marched in the track of our missionaries, and Count Bela Szechinyi, accompanied by Loczi and Kreitner, endeavoured to reach Lhassa. He had every possible document and letter of introduction; he was escorted by Chinese mandarins, and possessed a considerable fortune; but he could not get beyond Batang, and returned through the Yunnan. Cooper, having attempted to diverge from the beaten track of the missionaries, was murdered; while Baber merely followed the route they had mapped out, a good part of the information which his books contain being derived from members of the Thibet Mission. Not a single European coming from the East has been able to get as far as the tomb of Father Renou, but from the village where we disembark the route has been fully described as far as Tatsien-Lou by Father Desgodins, who is still hale and hearty. We shall be passing several spots where French blood has flowed with a disinterestedness not sufficiently admired, and as we shall be within a few miles of the spot where Father Brieux met with a cruel death, we regret not being numerous or well-armed enough to strike terror into the men who murdered him.

The great chief whom the Liang-tay, the paymaster-general at Batang, has sent to meet us is a Dungan, named Lishkünfan; and this Mussulman, who has regular features, is much more martial in appearance than his compatriots. Like most of his co-religionists, he thinks that his chief duty is to invoke Allah and abstain from eating pork in a country where it is difficult to get any other sort of meat, there being no mutton or yak-flesh except in places like Tatsien-Lou, where there are enough Mussulmans to have their own slaughter-house. He, however, is very regular in his ablutions, and his son, who has come with him, is also very natty in appearance. The father, who has the

GENERAL VIEW OF LITANG.

post of inspector of the troops, with a salary of about five pounds a month, has come to look through the accounts and satisfy himself that the garrison is in good trim.

After having drunk several cups of the fermented barley called *tchang*, and got " well on," he had the fifteen soldiers—ruffians with a cunning and degraded cast of countenance—drawn up in line, and proceeded to hold a court of justice in the open air. A bench was brought out and placed at the door of the barracks, covered with red cloth. When he had taken his seat, the captain of the archers sat on a stool beside him, while the soldiers were in a line to the left. The culprits were then brought forward, the first offender being a man who had been slandering others, including the wife of the captain. His calumnies had led to domestic unhappiness. The inspector in a voice of thunder shouts, " On your knees, sir ! " and down the wretch goes. Then the other soldiers are bidden to kneel and, after a few seconds, to get up again. The inspector eventually orders the culprit to receive six blows on the right cheek, and after a moment's hesitation three men come out from the ranks, two of them seizing him by the arms, while the other catches him by the pigtail and hits him six times on the cheek with a half-closed fist. As the punishment is being administered, the inspector gets more and more excited, positively howling at last, " Hit him six times on the mouth; that is where he gave offence." The punishment having been administered, the judge bids the soldiers be off; and they, having made a military salute to their chief, withdraw, the culprit coming up in turn and, with forehead touching the ground, thanking him sincerely for his goodness. The crowd disperses, the public appearing to be but little impressed by this scene, while the soldiers are scarcely able to restrain a smile, and the sufferer indulges in a grin.

In order to dissipate the painful impression which this affair has created, the inspector got up an entertainment for the evening, the whole of the women in the garrison being collected in the largest room of the place. *T-hang* was distributed freely, and the ladies sang and danced. As we had got down to a level of 3,300 feet the heat was rather trying, and the inspector, as drunk

LITANG: VIEW FROM THE ROOFS.

as Silenus, presided over the fête half-naked, seated on a platform in the posture of an idol. The dancing women as well as the singers were invited to partake of the drink, and the orgie lasted the best part of the night.

Such is a glimpse of the military customs of the Chinese in Thibet. I do not know how the army conducts itself at Pekin, but I may safely say that from Kuldja to the Red River we saw nothing bearing the faintest resemblance to discipline, or having any semblance of a sense of duty, while on many occasions we had proofs of cowardice. These men are only plucky when they are many against a few, and all they can do is to assassinate unarmed missionaries and isolated travellers.

A few miles beyond Tchoupalongue, on the route to Batang, we noticed a house at the entrance to a gorge, and learned that it was here Father Brieux was massacred, at the instigation

CHINESE FORT AT LITANG.

of the lamas and the Chinese. It seemed as if the Liang-tay was anxious to persuade us of the insecurity of this region, for we were greeted by salvos of musketry fired from the tops of the rocks, and a little farther on were accosted by a troop of ill-looking rascals, who seized our horses' reins and put out their hands for something in return for their salutes. Needless to say that we showed them our whips and did not give them a farthing.

No doubt these military demonstrations are intended to show that we are being well looked after. The authorities must be aware that we have heard of the murder of our compatriot Father Brieux, and think that we may have been sent to make an inquiry into that affair. Then, again, the dispersal of the Christian community of Batang, the devastation of their chapel, and the pillage of their houses, are still more recent, dating only from 1887. It is known that the Thibet Mission addressed a claim to the Tsong-li-Yamen through the French Minister—a claim which the Chinese Government promised to satisfy of course, but equally of course did not do so. The Liang-tay is aware how reprehensible the proceedings of the Chinese authorities are, and how much they deserve punishment, and public rumour has it that the object of our journey is to exact the reparation which is due, and to re-establish the Christians in possession of their lands.

When we reach Batang, situated in a pretty valley rich with harvest, we are treated as persons of distinction; honour is paid to us, and we are lodged in the newly-built Kouen-Khan, which is reserved for mandarins of high rank. The lamas, however, avoid us in the streets by running back, or taking refuge inside the houses; and when we make our way towards the lama-house, with its high walls, surmounted by a brilliant dome, the priests hasten to close the massive door, as if they were afraid of our penetrating into this so-called temple of wisdom, which is but a refuge for a set of good-for-nothings.

We paid several visits to the sites of the houses which were the legal property of the missionaries, and found the whole of them in ruins, like the chapel, between the walls of which the barley was sprouting. For the third season the Thibetans were about to reap the harvest in the fields of the mission without the Chinese authorities intervening, and one could not but ask what sort of a

Government this is to which European Powers appeal for redress, and with which they sign treaties only observed on one side. It is difficult to understand why we regard seriously the Emperor of China, who is not obeyed—either because he does not wish to be, or because he lacks the power to enforce his will. A power which is incapable of protecting anyone, or of applying the most insignificant rules of police, does not deserve the name of a Government, and I cannot understand the course taken by the nations of Europe.

Up to the present, murderers and fire-raisers have been going about here at Batang with perfect impunity; and yet the presence of a handful of well-armed men like ourselves suffices to make them feel uneasy.

Is it true that on the occasion of the Emperor's marriage all the diplomatists, with the exception of the Russian—though they do not, as a rule, agree among one another—asked to be allowed to offer their congratulations to the Emperor, and were refused? Is it true that when they attempted to make him presents, these presents were unceremoniously refused? Is it true that, after these rebuffs, they accepted the dinner which was contemptuously offered them? Is it true that they came in full dress, and were received by the chief of the Tsong-li-Yamen in undress, and in the room where all the tributary chiefs were massed together? Is it true that this latter proceeding is in the East—and in China more particularly—regarded as a peculiar display of disdain, and that it was not challenged as it should have been?

Perhaps I may have been misinformed, and for my own part I believe that our diplomatists are men of energy and prudence, careful of their country's interests, and of the strict observance of the Tientsin Treaty; and that if there are a great many matters still in suspense, it is simply because they cannot do everything at once.

It was to save them the trouble of reading a long report, and in order not to add to the number of cases still hung up, that we did not send them a formal complaint against the mandarin of Tatsien-Lou, who behaved to us like a good Chinaman, and who, owing to this, obtained as a permanency the post which he occupied temporarily.

At first we had some little differences at Batang with the Liang-tay, who insisted upon our showing him the papers we had asked for from Pekin, and which, as it appears, were sent to us through the Russian consul at Kashgar. But when we explained to him that, having been sent by this roundabout route, they must have gone astray, he appeared to be convinced that we had none, and let us go on without them.

On the 24th of June we reached Tatsien-Lou, having halted for a while at Litang. At Tatsien-Lou we were very cordially welcomed by Monsignor Biet, Fathers Dejean, Giraudot, etc., and by an English naturalist, Mr. Pratt, who will be able to confirm the statement that the missionaries rendered him every possible service without asking him what his religious creed was, any more than they asked as to ours. Mr. Pratt will be able also to say that the mandarin of Tatsien-Lou endeavoured to foment an attack upon us, under the grotesque pretence that we wanted to steal the treasures of the town.

I must relate the facts of this case in some detail. Let me premise by stating that the Tatsien-Lou missionaries had for the past two years been promised passports authorising them to return to Batang; but nothing had ever been done. So Monsignor Biet thought it as well to take advantage of our presence to open fresh negotiations with the mandarins of Fou Tchao Kong, and with the Liang-tay of Batang, Ouang Kia Yong, the latter being just now at Tatsien-Lou, on his way to his post. A council, at which we were all present, was held, and the mandarins promised the missionaries their passports, while the new treasurer undertook to let them go with him on

ENTRANCE TO THE TATSIEN-LOU VALLEY.

the seventeenth day of the moon. He even asked us for a revolver, in order that he might be able to intimidate the Thibetans; and he was promised one. The engagements entered into by the mandarins were not, of course, meant to be kept, and on the morning of the fifteenth day of the moon we were officially informed that Ouang Kia Yong would start the next day—that is to say, twenty-four hours sooner than had been agreed, and that there was no sign of any passport.

In the afternoon we sent Dedeken, in European dress, with the revolver that had been promised, and told him to get what information he could. He went to the door of the tribunal and handed in our cards, according to usage, and was told that the authorities were at table; so he was shown into an ante-room and kept waiting five hours, during which time, as the room was only divided from that in which the meal was being served by a thin partition, he could hear the Chinese insulting France and the other European countries, the voice of the mandarin Ouang Kia Yong being the loudest, so anxious was he that his insults should reach Father Dedeken's ears.

The festival lasted till nightfall, and then Tchao Kong, the mandarin of Tatsien-Lou, had the drum beaten through the town, and the crier was told to call out a man from each house, as the tribunal was in danger from the Europeans. So the people came rushing out—some armed with swords, others with bludgeons, and all with lanterns and umbrellas, for it was raining, fortunately, and this somewhat damped their ardour. We were unaware of all this, but, being uneasy as to the situation of our companion, sent two armed men to ask him to return. Father Dedeken was much surprised when he got outside to find the approaches to the Yamen blocked up by a large crowd. Followed by five or six hundred people, it suddenly occurred to him, on reaching the bridge across the stream, how likely they would be to throw him in, so he stopped, and in a loud tone, enjoined them not to follow him any farther. After a moment's hesitation the crowd turned back, and he was able to rejoin us in safety.

FRENCH MISSIONARIES.

These are the usual tactics of the mandarins for bringing about a massacre of Europeans, but they failed in this case for several reasons—one being that the population of Tatsien-Lou is chiefly composed of merchants, and is therefore of a peaceable disposition, while another was that the military chief, who is a Mussulman, and is on good terms with the missionaries, refused the 200 soldiers asked for. In the third place the Thibetan king would not move, out of antipathy to the Chinese.

The next day the Liang-tay, Ouang Kia Yong, started for Batang by a roundabout route; while the people of the Kuin-liangfou went about the bazaar insulting us, and saying that we were to be chained up and driven out like dogs, the missionaries sharing the same fate. The second man of the Kuinliangfou, one Lioupin, said that the Europeans must be killed, that he himself had massacred some at Tchong King, and that it was not a difficult matter. This, of course, was meant to frighten us.

The mandarin, finding that he had not attained his object, after waiting three or four days, sent a confidential adviser to us with apologies at the bishop's house. The messenger, who was attired in full dress, had his master's card in his hand, and said that the latter acknowledged himself to be solely responsible, but that action had been taken, by mistake, without his knowledge. Our reply was that we could only accept these apologies when the passports had been issued to the missionaries as a proof of his repentance being sincere. The mandarin, however, had not done with us yet, for, having arranged that some things should be stolen from us a few days after, he then pretended to take action against the culprits, when, in the presence of a large audience and by means of false witnesses and impudent fabrications, he sought to discredit us. Failing violence, he resorted to calumny. We lodged a complaint against him with his superior at Tcheng-tou-fou; but only for the form of the thing. And our complaint bore the usual fruit; that is to say, he was promoted after we had gone.

This is a good sample of the Chinese administration to which European Governments appeal for justice, and to which they look for loyal conduct. To do so is sheer waste of time, for these people are cowards, and are moved solely by fear. As I write these lines the war vessels of European Powers are collected in Chinese waters, and are awaiting the result of the negotiations of their diplomatists with the Chinese, and it is easy to predict what the outcome of all this will be. The mandarins will apologise and pay an indemnity, they will make certain custom-house concessions, and a few ruffians who ought to have been executed long ago will have their heads cut off. And so the comedy will end, while the mandarins are congratulated by their superiors and promoted, the people being told that the Europeans are always ready to sell their lives for money, and that they make threats which they never carry out.

We stayed more than a month at Tatsien-Lou to recruit our strength before going on to Tonquin. That we were able to carry out this last part of our programme is due to the kindness of our compatriots.

During our journey we had formed several collections intended for French museums, and at Tatsien-Lou they had been considerably augmented by purchases which our fellow-countrymen had put us in the way of making. Had it been necessary to convey all this through Tonquin, it is doubtful whether we should ever have got through; but, fortunately for us, Mr. Pratt offered to take charge of our baggage until he reached the first French consulate, which, as we calculated, would be at Hankau, while we sent our photographs through the English consul at Tchung-King, whose name I regret not having by me, so that I might publicly thank him. Photographs and collections alike reached Europe in good condition, and have since been exhibited in the Paris Museum of Natural History, where they will at present remain. Mr. Pratt was obliged to have our packages carried for a month overland, and then to purchase junks and go down the Yan-tse-Kiang as far as

Shanghai, for our consul at Hankau being absent, Mr. Pratt was kind enough to go on with them. At Shanghai he went to M. Wagner, the French consul, who declined to have anything to do with the matter, and he then applied to the procurator of the foreign missions, who saw them on board the steamer for Marseilles. Thanks to Mr. Pratt, we knew that the fruits of our long journey were as safe as the perils of navigation on the Yan-tse-Kiang admitted, and so we felt that we could make for Tonquin without any encumbrances. We should have left Tatsien-Lou sooner, but we heard on the 13th of July that some Europeans, who had started from Sining-fou, were coming. However, after vainly waiting a week for them, we left by the route which Baber, the English traveller, had followed. It was the 28th of July when we bade good-bye to the members of the Thibet Mission, whom we cannot thank too much for their cordial hospitality, and from whom travellers who may be brought into this region by the passion for exploration are sure of receiving disinterested assistance, valuable information, and advice dictated by consummate prudence and experience. Mr. Pratt, I am quite sure, is of the same opinion, as well as Mr. Rokkill (?), the American diplomatist, who made such a daring journey from the Koukou-Nor to the Tatsien-Lou, by way of Jyékounda.

It is with a heavy heart that we say good-bye to our fellow-countrymen, wishing them all success in their arduous enterprise. We determine to note carefully the residences of the other missionaries which we shall pass on the way, as being so many oases in the vast desolation of China. When we leave Tatsien-Lou we leave Thibet, and from the very first stage the eye wanders over moist valleys inhabited by a very dense population which utilises every handful of vegetable soil, and even manages to grow a few heads of corn in the corners of rocks, and upon the stony sides of the mountains. Village succeeds village with painful sameness. The pagodas are half to pieces, and as you enter the village you see figures of gods painted in bright colours but crumbling to pieces, and then comes a sort of triumphal arch on which are inscribed moral phrases like those of schoolchildren's copy-books. The streets are infested by yelping curs and dirty pigs wallowing in the mud; by children as dirty as the animals; by women with legs the size of a chair rail, and feet like snuff-boxes, and by porters or mules carrying heavy loads. The inns are horrible dens impregnated with the most varied odours, that of opium not being the least unpleasant. These inns have the most pompous names, such as the "Polar Star," the Chinese having a great weakness for the four cardinal points. The staple articles of food are rice and pork, and eggs and chickens are to be had in villages, omelettes being made with the former, and soup with the latter; and fish is also eaten, caught with the aid of cormorants, which, flung into the water from a boat, catch the fish and bring them to the fisher after the manner of a retriever.

We cannot but be struck by the economy of the people, their parsimony, their avarice, their art in turning literally everything to account. Thus they make lamp wicks out of the heart of a certain kind of rush, and they also use this for cupping. They have a way of supplying what is wanting in the products of industry with a skill of hand and a patience beyond all belief, and if they did not smoke they would not indulge in a single superfluity. It might even be argued that the opium-smoker does not indulge in a superfluity, since he eats and drinks less than the non-smoker. In this land of hunger, where the struggle for existence renders people so ferocious and pitiless, the essential thing is to keep body and soul together, and I have seen men dropping from inanition on the roadway and the Chinese stepping over them without offering to give them assistance. The famishing wretch might die, and his body would lie there without anyone taking notice of it.

In the regions we traversed before reaching Yunnan, we

FISHING WITH CORMORANTS.

saw no display of the sentiment which certain people call altruism. In these populous regions of the Setchouen no one has time to think of others, the difficulty of getting a bare subsistence being so great that it seems to have hardened men's hearts towards their fellows.

Our carriers are poor wretches who have been recruited specially for the work, and have scarcely a rag upon their bodies. They feed on dried biscuits, Indian corn cooked in oil, and what rice is to be had at inns on the roadside. But they all have their opium-pipe, and when the imperious need for the drug begins to make itself felt, they quicken their steps so as to reach the inn where the contractor is awaiting them with the opium which constitutes the bulk of their pay. These inns, in which we try to sleep, are, however, so infested with vermin that we cannot, as a rule, close our eyes; so we even look back with regret upon those of Thibet, which at the time seemed so revolting. We are much struck by the enormous loads of tea carried by men over very steep paths. It appears that these men belong to families in which the occupation is hereditary, and that they form a corporation.

At Fou-lin we quit the high road, which goes on east, and make our way towards the Yunnan over the highlands of the Tien Shan. On the road we come upon Chinese towns and villages formed chiefly of emigrants from the Setchouen, the mountain being inhabited by the Lolos, a tall race of men with long feet, very energetic and warlike, and inspiring great terror among the Chinese, whom they rob whenever they get the chance.

The Chinese whom we encounter in this district appear to be a most wretched set of beings, very small, eaten up with fever, and disfigured by enormous goitres. They are, as a rule, inoffensive, but we meet with occasional difficulties in the populous places, the inhabitants sometimes insulting us, and throwing stones at the doors of the inn where we are lodging, although, on these occasions, the mandarins tell us that we are quite safe within the precincts of their tribunal. We inform the crowd that, if one of them dares to lay hands on us, we shall

LOLOS.

shoot him, while the mandarins are told that we shall hold them responsible for any blood shed. This has the desired effect; and it is the same with the future bachelors of letters whom we meet on the road, this being the period for examinations, for although

THE RED RIVER.

they are often more numerous than we are, and apply very insulting expressions to us, we never hesitate to use our sticks, and keep them in their place. We would rather die than let ourselves insulted; and it was by acting upon this feeling at all risks that we were able to go along the banks of the Red River, after a halt at Yunnan-Fou and another at Mong-tse, where our consul, M. Leduc, and the Europeans employed in the custom-house received us very cordially.

We embarked upon the Red River, which well deserves its name, on the 22nd of September, having, since we left the frontier of Siberia, travelled nearly 3,750 miles either on foot or on horseback, so it will be readily understood how delighted we were to stretch ourselves on the junk which M. Jansen, the Danish telegraph engineer, had engaged for us. On the evening of that day we were at the post of Bac-Sat, on French soil, and on the 25th at Lao-kai, where M. Laroze gave us a very friendly reception, and where we changed our junk. This was but the prelude to many more such receptions during our progress through the colony, while at Hanoï itself M. Raoul Bonnal and General Bichot were most cordial, as indeed was the whole population of Tonquin, to whom we here tender our sincere thanks. If we were struck by the beauty of the Red River, not less so were we by the comfort and liveliness of Hanoï; while from what we saw of the delta—of the wealth of vegetation, and the extreme fertility of an inexhaustible soil—we could only conclude that this is a colony out of which a great deal may be made. All that is needed is that an agreement should be arrived at concerning this child, whose advent, being rather unexpected, upset certain calculations and plans. But he, I believe, has a future, and will make his way in the world if proper care is taken of him.

Every one is aware that it is easier and quicker to get back from Tonquin by sea than to traverse the ancient continent of

Asia in order to get to it. For the return voyage we embarked at Haiphong, and so by Hong-Kong to Marseilles. At Hong-Kong we sent our Chinaman back to his native land; he was to

LAO-KAI.

return in company with some Belgian missionaries. That vain little fellow Abdullah, who has some good qualities all the same, left us at Port Saïd, while Rachmed was to accompany us to Paris before returning to Russian Turkestan, and Father Dedeken is going to spend a little time in Belgium. Before laying down the pen, I would add that we are all very well satisfied with the results of our journey, and must thank my companions for the confidence they reposed in me, and for having worked with all their might to carry out a somewhat daring scheme. We have all done the best we could: we hope we may be excused for not having done more.

RACHMED AND A THIBETAN INNKEEPER.

THE END.

INDEX.

Abdallah, Villages of, I. 79, 82, 88, 89, 102, 104, 105, 106, 116.
Abdullah, interpreter, I. 6, 23, 43, 57, 64, 75, 79, 82; makes an exchange with Kunshi Khan Beg, 89; 96, 112, 142, 144, 156, 166; lost in a storm, 199; and the sources of Brahma - Pootra, 217; interview with Thibetan chiefs, II. 15; and the ambassadors from Lhassa, 38; drinks the Amban's spirits, 90; 220.
Agricultural implements of Thibetans, II. 143.
Abiligane, I., 68.
Akker, Village of, II. 166.
Aktarma, I. 62, 63; characteristics of the people of, 64; migration, and primitive implements of the inhabitants of, 65.
Almonds, I. 46.
Altars to Buddha, I. 36.
Altitude of mountains, Enormous, I. 207.
Altyn Tagh, The, I. 104, 113, 128; appearance of, 132, 173.
Amban Ashkan Dawan, Pass of, I. 156, 159, 163; ascent of the, 167.
Amban of Lhassa, The, II. 37, 39, 41-45; tent of, 50; salutes the travellers in French, 80; hospitality of, 83.
Andidjan, I. 58.
Antelopes, I. 67; II. 27, 100.
Apple-trees, I. 20, 42.
Apricot-trees, I. 20, 42.
Aqueducts for irrigating fields, II. 154.
Ara, II. 179.
Archan Buluk spring, I. 35.
Arkan, Characteristics and wretched condition of the people of, I. 69.
Arkars, I. 30, 164, 204.
Arrack, II. 46.
Aryk River, I. 117.
Ata, Ismail, I. 98.
Atentze, II. 188.
Attagout Agha, I. 97.

Ba, II. 167.
Baber, missionary in Thibet, II. 196, 211.
Bac-Sat, II. 219.
Bagh Tokai encampment, I. 156.
Balgoun Louk, Encampment at, I. 163.
Baratchdin, I. 76, 103.
Barantashis (horse stealers), I. 20.
Barberries, I. 12.
Barkhans, I. 183; demolished by a tempest, 196.

Barley, purchased at Kourla, I. 43; grown at Aktarma, 65.
Bata-Soumdo, II. 117, 118.
Batang, I. 6, 111, 158; II. 153; destruction of the mission at, 175, 202; treatment of the travellers at, 202-204.
Bazaars at Kourla, I. 42, 43.
Beard, Signs made with the, I. 127, 172.
Bears, II. 96, 101, 159, 163.
Beggars at So, II. 111.
Bela-Szechny, Count, I. 6; II. 196.
Bichat, General, II. 219.
Biet, Monsignor, and the Batang mission, II. 85, 175; his reception of the travellers at Tatsien-Lou, 204.
Birch-trees, I. 58; II. 153.
Birds in the desert, I. 72, 78.
Black-tree, The, I. 39.
Blue River, I. 205; II. 194.
Boars, I. 25, 69, 102.
Bokalik, I. 117, 136; gold mines in the neighbourhood of, 164.
Bokhara, I. 52.
Bones, A valley of, I. 206.
Bonnal, M. Raoul, II. 219.
Bonvalot, M., reference to by Prince Henry of Orleans, I. 75, 76, 108, 109.
Borokusté River, The, I. 31.
Botchou River, II. 99.
Bongou Bashi, I. 72.
Boulak Bashi, I. 140.
Bouran, The, I. 193.
Bread at Kourla, I. 43.
Briars, II. 144.
Brieux, Father, Murder of, II. 196, 201.
Bridge of Sougomba, II. 154.
Brigands, Chinese treatment of, I. 11; seizing the travellers' horses, II. 193.
Broom, Prickly, I. 63.
Brushwood, II. 112, 116, 120.
Buddha: Images of, used for healing purposes, I. 16; statue of, in a Lama monastery, 18; altars to, 36; images placed with engraved prayers under trees, II. 80; consecration of males to, 155.
Buddhism, I. 10; and the transmigration of the soul, 14; inscriptions on mountains, 31.
Burben-cho Ré Mountains, II. 20, 25.
Burben-cho, Salt deposit at, II. 11, 16, 19, 20.
Burial customs, I. 101.

Camels, I. 26; indications of approaching death in, 29; feeding on yantag, 36; crossing a river on a raft, 60; terrify natives, 69; wild, 82, 87; mounting the Koum Dawan, 140; crossing the ice, 172; blinded by sand, 196; death from exhaustion, II. 33.
Camp de la Miséricorde, I. 180.
Cañon, Picturesque, near the Koum Dawan, I. 134.
Caravan, Organisation of a, I. 4.
Carbuncles caused by the cold, I. 166.
Carey the traveller, I. 1, 62, 111, 112, 126, 131, 146, 159.
Catu, The Thibetan, II. 41, 152.
Catholic ritual, Relics of, at Lhassa, II. 85.
Cuwerdak, I. 78.
Celibacy, Vow of, II. 155.
Cemetery at Abdallah, I. 102, 103.
Chamois of the Himalaya, The, I. 205.
Changka, II. 174, 176; reception of the travellers at, 178; the lamas of, 184.
Chartres, Duc de, I. 2.
Cherry-trees, II. 153.
Children, Mortality of, I. 100; offered to Moloch, II. 155; sandals of, 194.
China, Valleys of, I. 2; emigration in, 8; filthiness of inns in, II. 192, 212, 215.
Chinese, Perfidy of, towards Europeans, I. 49; taxes levied by, 67, 89, 164; thieving propensities of the, 97; their obstinacy and pride, 167; their heartlessness, 188, 212; at Bata-Samdo, II. 117; clannishness of, 123; soldiers at Houmda, 149; their unfeeling disposition contrasted with the kindness of heart of the Thibetans, 164, 165; ferocity of the children, 165; mode of salutation, 167; adepts in compliments, 169; specimens of soldiers, 171; their futile promises, 175, 180; soldiers useless in Thibet, 191; punishments, 199; lack of discipline in the army, 201; powerlessness of the emperor, 203; contemptuous treatment of foreign diplomatists, 203; insults to foreign countries, 207; their cowardice, 210; their parsimony and avarice, 212; hatred of foreigners, 215.
Chinese governor, Hospitality of, I. 7.
Chinese servants, I. 6.
Clematis, II. 194.
Coins, Thibetan, II. 108.
Cold, intense, I. 202, 210, II. 1, and *passim*.
Columbus Mountains, I. 173, 175, 179.
Cones, Lake of, I. 203.
Cones of ice, I. 211.
Cooper, missionary in Thibet, II. 196.
Copper mine near the Kunges, I. 19.
Corn, Grinding, I. 91.
Couznetzoff, I. 76, 102.
Cranes, II. 95.
Crossoptilons, II. 147.
Crows with "metallic croak," I. 215, 217.

Csoma the Hungarian, and his Thibetan dictionary, II. 195.
Curlews, II. 144.

Dala Pass, II. 144.
Dâlgleish the traveller, I. 159.
Dam, Pass of, II. 46, 96.
Dameloune Mountains, II. 187.
Dancers, Thibetan, II. 135.
Dandelion, I. 217.
Détchou River, II. 147.
Dedeken, Father, Belgian missionary, I. 5, 6, 75, 76, 83, 97, 120, 150, 158; amusing interview with a Dungan, 161, 172, 175; at the burial of Ninz, 193: 200; II. 13; and the Thibetan chief, 19; taken for a Chinaman, 20; 140; and the mandarins of Tatsien-Lou, 207; 220.
Deer, I. 25; II. 120, 147, 154.
Dejean, Father, II. 204.
Desert, Fascination of life in the, I. 24; birds in the, 72; solitude of the, 77; reed grass, and blue pools of the, 78; journey through the, 163.
Desert-sickness, I. 131.
Desgodins, Father, II. 85, 177, 188, 195, 196.
Deutschmé, I. 98; II. 144.
Di-Ti, II. 72, 77.
Diogenes of Velasquez, The, II. 20.
Divers, Black, II. 96.
Djashas, The, II. 67, 73.
Djahan Saï River, I. 132; granite in the valley of the, 133, 143.
Djala Mountains, II. 147.
Djankalo (Changka), II. 167.
Djarkent, I. 3; recruiting men at, 4; start from, 4; 9; II. 32.
Djancounnene, II. 96.
Djiddas, I. 63.
Dogs, the travellers' watchmen, II. 13, 30; of Thibetans, 96; at So, 111; 128.
Dotou, II. 167; the lama-house, and prayer-mills at, 170.
Duck, Red, I. 88, note.
Ducks, Flesh of, I. 96, II. 95.
Dungans, The, I. 42, 44, 70, 169.
Dupleix Mountains, I. 206, 207.
Dust, Clouds of, assuming singular shapes, II. 78.
Dzérine, II. 160, 163.

Eagles, Black, I. 199; II. 100.
Edelweiss, I. 28, 212.
Eglantines, II. 194.
Electrical phenomenon, II. 114.
Elephants, I. 61.
Elms, I. 38.
Emigration in China, I. 8.
Eutin, I. 95.
Extortions of Thibetan chiefs, II. 116.
Eyes, Inflammation of the, through a hurricane, 195.

Fage, Father, II. 177, 195.
Falcons, I. 199.
Fat mixed with bread, I. 43; for frost-bitten foot, 196.
Feet, Frost-bitten, I. 196.
Ferghana, The, I. 40, 44, 58.
Ferrier Mountain, I. 188.
Fieldfares, I. 67.
Figs, I. 42.
Fir-trees, II. 144; forests of, 147.
Flour purchased at Kourla, I. 43.
Fording a river, Novel mode of, II. 134.
Forests on mountains, I. 23.
Fossils at 19,000 feet, I. 209.
Fou-lin, II. 215.
Foxes, I. 135, 188; II. 163.
Frost-bitten feet, I. 196.
Frozen geysers, I. 211, 215.
Frozen meat, I. 211.

Gabet, missionary, I. 111, 203; II. 36, 177, 195.
Garments made from the *tchiga* plant, I. 68; from wild hemp, 91.
Gashar, I. 97.
Gatine, II. 92, 93.
Gazelles, I. 23, 69, 79, 133, 135.
Geese, Wild, I. 78, 88 (note); II. 95.
Géodes, I. 76.
Geographical Society of England, I. 111.
Geysers, Frozen, I. 211, 215.
Ghadik River, I. 38.
Gill, English explorer in Thibet, II. 195.
Giometchou River, II. 152; breadth at Lamda, 154
Girmudot, Father, II. 204.
Goats of nomads, II. 94.
Gobi Desert, Mongolia, The, I. 62, 128.
Goitres, II. 116, 156, 215.
Gold said to be found at Kizil Sou River, I. 136.
Gold mines in the neighbourhood of Bokalik, I. 164.
Goumbous, I. 62.
Granite in the valley of the Djahan-Saï, I. 133.
Grapes, I. 42.
Grass of the highlands, Peculiar character of the, I. 212; drying, II. 114.
Gratou, unsociability of inhabitants, II. 139.
Greediness of Thibetans, II. 5.
Grottoes, II. 144.
Gulls, White, II. 95.

Haïphong, II. 219.
Hami, Oasis of, I. 44.
Handglasses given to natives, II. 30.
Hannibal crossing the Rhône, I. 61.
Hanoï, II. 219.
Hares, I. 67, 108, 109, 163, 165, 168, 203, 210.
Haschisch, Smoking, I. 114, 149.
Hassar, Village of, II. 163; a street in, 164.
Hastings, Lord, I. 41.

Headache relieved by snow, II. 116.
Hemp, I. 20.
Henry, Prince, of Orléans, I. 2, 6; kills a stag, 28; photographs a lama, 30; photographs some Torgots, 38; 46; threatened with arrest at Kourla, 49; 116; 120; perilous position of, 135; 147; 158; 172; 174; 175; 178; finds the track of Kalmuck pilgrims, 194; leads the camels, 195, 196; 197; kills two *orongos*, 200; kills a yak, 205; 212; photographs the first Thibetan native encountered by the travellers, II. 2; photographs a Thibetan dwelling, 24; 220.
Hermit, Dwelling of a, II. 95.
Honeymoon before marriage, II. 134.
Hong-Kong, II. 219.
Hop-vines, I. 20.
Horse-stealing by the Kirghis, I. 27.
Horses, Fastening up, in the desert, I. 77; instinct of, 84, 108; lost on the mountains, 181; effect of frost on the eyes of, 195; death of, from over-drinking, 206; loss of strength from cold, 212; feeding on raw flesh, II. 67; cleverness of, 101; of Tsonron, 173.
Hot springs, I. 205, 211, 217; II. 35, 159.
Houmla, II. 149.
Hounds, I. 125.
Houses, Material used in the construction of, II. 149, 154; decorations on, 191.
Huc, Father, his narratives of travel, I. 2, 111; 203; II. 26, 36; and the relics of Catholic ritual in Thibet, 85; 177, 195.
Huns, The, and their horses, I. 61.
Huts of Thibetans, II. 114.
Hydromel, II. 122.

Ia-La Mountain, II. 103, 108.
Iabshou plant, The, I. 174, 211.
Iça, servant to the travellers, I. 114, 149; II. 90.
Ice, Cones of, I. 211.
Ili, Province of, I. 7; fertility of, 7; its transference to China, 8; emigration from, 9; and the Torgots, 35, 46; sheep of, 71.
Images of Buddha used for healing purposes, I. 16; deposited on *obos*, 31; given to Thibetans, II. 140.
Imatch, camel-driver, I. 26; his reflections about camels and sheep, 71; 112, 141, 196; his feet frost-bitten, II. 7; illness of, 25; his death, 31.
Inns, Chinese, Filthiness of, II. 192, 212, 215.
Instinct of a horse, I. 84.
Intchigué-Darya River, The, I. 62.
"Invisible horsemen," I. 216.
Iron manufactory at Lagoun, II. 150.
Ithaginis, II. 153.

Jasmine, II. 194.
Jujube-trees, I. 38, 68.
Junipers, II. 35, 107, 112, 115, 116, 144, 147.

Kabchiguć-gol, Defile of, I. 31; meaning of word, 32.
Kala Mountain, II. 155.
Kalmucks, The: their characteristics and harsh treatment by the Kirghis, I. 10; and the Torgots, 35; and the inhabitants of Aktarma, 64; 103, 148, 176, 194; II. 13.
Kama, The, I. 3.
Kampir plant, The, I. 174.
Kara Koum, The, I. 62.
Karakoutchoun, I. 97, 98.
Kara Bourane River, I. 107, 109.
Karakoyuk, I. 98.
Karashar, Lake of, I. 38; Governor of, and the travellers, 47, 51; 103.
Kara Shote, I. 146.
Kargalik (Tcharkalik), I. 97, 98.
Karimeta, II. 143.
Kash, The, I. 8, 11.
Kashgar, Emigrants from, I. 8; 9; governed by Yakoob-Beg, 40.
Kela Mountains, II. 116.
Kemczetiantché Lake, I. 107.
Ken-Si, II. 108, 123.
Kérémata, Abdu, I. 80.
Khan of the Torgots, The, II. 43.
Khiva, I. 52.
Khotan, I. 98.
Kin-sha-Kiang River, II. 194.
Kirghis, Siberian, I. 9; their depredations on Kalmucks, 10; wearing tablets as passports, 11; formation of their skulls, 14; source of livelihood, and cheerfulness, 20; addicted to horse-stealing, 27; feuds with the Mongols, 28; their broad faces, 58; 66.
Kissing amongst natives, I. 127.
Kitchou River, II. 190.
Kizil Sou River, I. 111, 116, 121; gold said to be found at, 136.
Kontché-Darya, The, I. 40, 42, 57, 58; raft for crossing the, 60.
Koushou, II. 186, 187.
Koukou Nor, I. 203.
Koukou Nor River, I. 111; II. 77.
Koukounmanes, I. 143.
Koul toukmit Koul, Plain of, I. 63.
Koulans, I. 133, 147, 165, 174, 177, 205; II. 27.
Koum Dawan Mountain, I. 134, 140.
Kountsétinne, II. 191.
Kourla, I. 40, 41; general appearance, and the people of, 42; the travellers threatened with arrest at, 47; start of the caravan from, 52; chiefs of, and the travellers, 55-57; 98; 111.
Koushoune, II. 159.
Kreitner, explorer in Thibet, II. 196.
Kuldja, I. 4; Russian consul at, 6; 39, 58, 112, 120.
Kunshap Khan, I. 92.
Kunges, Valley of the, I. 12, 19.
Kunshi Khan Beg, I. 82, 84, 89.
Kuntchi Khan, a Lob chief, I. 132.

Lagoun, II. 149; iron manufactory at, 150.
Lake of Cones, I. 203.
Lake Montcalm, I. 205, 206.
Lama, Grand, Description of a, and his reception of travellers, I. 15, 16.
Lamaism, Supposed derivation of, II. 143.
Lamas, Tents of the, I. 13, 18, 83; appearance of the, II. 42; chanting prayers and blowing trumpets, 51, 52; makers of medicine, 53; travelling, 101, 102; of the monastery of So, 106; training-school for, 117; initiation of, 126; mendicant, 132; of Karimeta, 141; female, 142; house of, at Djala Pass, 148; of Ouoshishoune, 160; house at Dzérine, 163; house at Dotou, 167; of Changka, 183.
Lamda, II. 152, 153; the Giomtchou River at, 154.
Lamé, II. 152.
Lammergeiers, II. 35, 53, 102.
Landscape, A typical Pomeranian, I. 65.
Lao-kai, II. 219.
Larks, I. 67, 178, 182, 199, 211; II. 80, 93.
Laroze, M., II. 219.
Latchou River, II. 159.
Leduc, M., French consul at Mong-tsc, II. 219.
Leindünne, II. 188.
Lendjoune, II. 166.
Lepsinsk, I. 20.
Lhassa, Supplications brought from, I. 15 statue of Grand Lama of, 16; 19, 103; route to, by the Kizil Sou, 111; pilgrims from, 155; 218; II. 6, 7, 8, 18; the "city of spirits," 33; ambassadors from, 36, 37; the Amban of, 37-45; visit to the travellers at Dam of chiefs from, 55; a hotbed of intrigue, 69; presents for the travellers from, 84; reputed resort of countless pilgrims, 188.
Lilac-trees, II. 155.
Liquorice-plants, I. 12, 20, 38.
Litang, II. 204.
Lob Nor, The, I. 4, 49, 51, 52, 62, 63, 73; journey to, 76; characteristics of the people in, 80; the great "lake" of, 90, 109; work of the sand at, 99, 110, 206.
Lobi chiefs refuse aid to the travellers, I. 122.
Lobis, The, I. 144, 145, 169, 170.
Loczi, explorer in Thibet, II. 196.
Lolos, The, II. 215.
Lorin, Henri, I. 2.
Lottery, A singular, near Sérésumdo, II. 132.

Macaroni, Chinese, I. 84.
Madman at Bata-Soumdo, The, and the mirror, II. 118.
Mahomet, Festival of, at Tcharkalik, I. 115.
Maktchou River, II. 167.
Malthusianism, Religious, II. 155.
Mandalik, I. 146.
Mandarins, The, and passports for foreigners, I. 6; enticing Russian peasants to settle in

INDEX.

Chinese territory, 9; of Kourla, 44; threatening travellers, 57; from Lhassa, 56; of Changka, II. 178.
Mardjan Agha, I. 97.
Marriage customs, I. 100, 105; II. 122-127, 134.
Marseilles, II. 219.
Massacre of Thibetans by the Sopkou, II. 165.
Mazar, I. 8, 9, 11.
Meat, Frozen, I. 211.
Mekong River, II. 152.
Melons, I. 39, 42, 46, 64.
Mendicant lamas, II. 132.
Mesny, explorer in Thibet, II. 196.
Mienshari, I. 97.
Mill, Thibetan, II. 23.
Mirages, due to salt, I. 76, 108, 126, 168; II. 16.
Mission, Destruction of the Batang, II. 175, 202.
Monastery, Lama, I. 15, 16, 18; at So, II. 93, 105, 112.
Money-lender at So, A, II. 108, 111.
Mong-tse, II. 219.
Mongols, Physiognomy of, I. 10; method of threshing wheat, 12; tea-drinking of, 16; poverty and uncleanliness, and the ugliness of the women, 19; their feuds with the Kirghis, 28; physical traits, 35, 97; II. 156.
Monkeys, I. 210; II. 96, 156.
Montcalm Lake, I. 205, 206.
Moscow, I. 3.
Moula Kourghan, I. 163.
Mountain sickness, I. 141, 142, 166; remedy for, 166, 183.
Mountains covered with forests, I. 23; with surface of salt, 30; Buddhist inscription on, 31; a wilderness of, 198-218; like waves, 204; Dupleix, 206, 207; enormous altitude of, 207.
Music and dancing at Tchinagi, I. 59.
Musk-deer, II. 120, 147, 154.
Mutton, Salted, at Kourla, I. 43.

Nain-Singh, the pundit, II. 34.
Namtso, I. 158, 218; II. 8, 11, 23; description of, 33; arrival of travellers at, 34; the "Heavenly Lake," 54.
Naptchou, The, II. 77, 92.
Natural History Museum, Paris, and the collection of M. Bonvalot, I. 206 (note).
Nia, I. 164.
Niaz, Death and burial of, I. 191-193.
Nigan, II. 83.
Nijni-Novgorod, I. 3.
Nilka, The, I. 12.
Ningling Tangla, II. 8, 11, 12, 27, 32; striking appearance of, 33, 74.
Nionma, or turnip, II. 115; cattle fed with, 143.
Nouniaz Agha, I. 97.

Oak-trees, II. 172.
Obo Pass, I. 143.

Obos, I. 31, 32. 168, 210; II. 99, 128, 103; enormous specimen at Tchoungo, 143; 187.
Oil, Sesamum, I. 43.
Ointment on the faces of Thibetans, II. 5.
Omdjamtchou River, II. 100.
Omsk, I. 3.
Omtchou River, II. 99.
Opium-smoking, II. 108, 212.
Orongos, I. 178, 188, 194, 201.
Orosses (Russians), I. 35.
Ouloug Koul, I. 66; reception of travellers by the chief of, 67.
Onoshishoune, II. 159; lamas of, 160.
Ourga, II. 52.
Ourounitchi, I. 47, 159.
Ourtchou River, II. 92, 99, 100.
Ouzoun Tchor River, I. 146, 149.

Pa-Lan (i.e., English or Russians), II. 14, 15.
Pashalik, I. 146.
Pagoda of a Lama monastery, Description of a, I. 18; at Djala Pass, II. 147.
Palao-meat, I. 28, 144, 163, 211.
Pamir, The, I. 2, 41; II. 27, 102.
Pansies, I. 28.
Parasols of Chinese soldiers, II. 178.
Paris, Route to Tonquin from, I. 2; exhibition of, 2, 3.
Parpa, servant of the travellers, I. 43, 44; beats natives of Arkan, 70; 112; 117; 156; 170; II. 25, 90.
Partridges, I. 35, 142, 165, 168, 210; II. 113, 154.
Passports, I. 6; amongst the Kirghis, 11; demanded at Kourla, 46; shown to a Thibetan chief, II. 19; for missionaries at Tatsien-Lou, 204.
Peat pits, I. 30.
Pekin, I. 112.
Pelisse of Thibetan, II. 2, 18.
Pepper-trees, I. 20.
Petchili, Gulf of, I. 41.
Petzoff, Russian traveller, I. 73.
Pheasants, in the valley of the Kunges, I. 12; 67, 153; II. 163.
Phenomenon, Electric, II. 114.
Photographing a lama, I. 30; some Torgots, 38.
Pickpockets at Kourla, I. 51.
Pigeons, II. 27.
Pigtails of Thibetans, II. 8.
Pilgrims, I. 150, 155; camp of, 195, 196; II. 133.
Pine forests, II. 156, 173.
Pipes for smoking, Thibetan, II. 114.
Pirojki, I. 84.
Ploughing, Methods of, II. 112, 164.
Poioundo, II. 120.
Poisoned rivers, I. 68.
Polyandry, II. 124.
Polygamy, II. 124, 126.
Pomeranian landscape, A typical, I. 65.
Ponies of Thibetans, II. 5.
Poplars in the valley of the Kunges, I. 12;

20; forest of, 59; 62, 68; at Talkitchin, 71; 108; II. 155, 166.
Poptchou River, II. 100.
Porphyry, I. 168.
Portrait drawn by a lama, II. 130.
Poula, II. 186.
Pratt, Mr., English collector at Tatsien-Lou, II. 204, 210, 211.
Prayer-mills, II. 27, 99, 128; at Dotou, 170; 183.
Prayers of Buddhists, I. 18, 37; written on canvas and on slabs, and left at *obos*, 31; at burials, 101; on tents, II. 12; engraved on schist, 23, 79; written on stones, 26, 128; chanted by lamas, 51, 141; turned by windmills, 143; for rain, 184, 185.
Prjevalsky, the traveller, I. 1, 2, 6, 19, 40, 41, 46, 62, 79, 82, 88 (note), 89; and the Lake of Lob Nor, 90; 97 (note); 99, 107, 111, 126, 168; and the Columbus Mountains, 173; and the Koukou route, 203; II. 95, 195.
Pumpkins, I. 91.

Rachmed, I. 3, 4, 6, 28; opinion of the Chinese, 46; 52, 108, 115, 119; beats a Lobé chief, 122; 125, 144, 149, 155, 167, 171; lost on the mountains, 184; his sage advice to the travellers, 207; stoned by Thibetans, II. 140; 220.
Rachmed, Ata, I. 57, 58.
Raft for crossing the Kontché-Darya, I. 61.
Raisins purchased at Kourla, I. 43.
Raspberries, I. 12; II. 155, 173.
Rats of the mountains, I. 199; II. 80.
Reclus Volcano, The, I. 188.
Red River, The, II. 219; beauty of, 219.
Red soil near Akker, II. 166.
Reed grass, I. 78.
Reeds in the Tarim, I. 92.
Renou, Father, II. 174, 177, 195, 196.
Rheumatism cured at Archan Buluk spring, I. 35; attacking women, 100; marmot fat as a cure for, 117.
Rhododendrons, II. 120, 144, 147, 153.
Rhubarb plant, The, I. 212, 217.
Richthofen, the traveller, I. 6.
Ritchimbo, II. 115.
River, Novel mode of fording a, II. 134.
Rivers poisoned by vegetable matter, I. 68.
Rokkill (?), Mr., American diplomatist, II. 211.
Rontéoundo, II. 156.
Rontchi, II. 144.
Ruins of dwellings near Sérésoundo, II. 131; in the valley of the Mahtchou, 165.
Ruysbroek Volcano, named after the Flemish traveller, I. 194, 198.

Saia, Meaning of, I. 119.
Sakis, or tents for the winter, I. 38.
Saksaoul, I. 131, 133.
Salt on mountains, I. 30; mixed with bread, 43; on the roads, 65; on the banks of the Tarim, 69; at Talkitchin, 71; on the road to Lob, 76; ponds, 92; on the Ouzoun Tchor, 146; in the desert, 174; of Burhen-cho, II. 11.
Saltpetre, I. 97, 109.
Salutation, Thibetan modes of, II. 2, 8, 18, 48, 98.
Samarkand, I. 4, 7.
Samda Kansain Mountains, II. 68, 74.
Samda-Tchou River, II. 68.
Sand, Waves of, I. 174; fantastic scene from, 196.
Sandhills, I. 62, 63, 67, 72, 175, 196.
Sarthians of Turkestan, I. 58, 66.
Sasan, a chief of the Kirghis, I. 20.
Satchou, II. 155.
Schist, Prayers engraved on, II. 23, 79.
Sétchou River; II. 147, 148.
Setchouen, I. 151; II. 212.
Semipalatinsk, I. 3, 58.
Sérésoundo, II. 130.
Shanghai, I. 5.
Shaven heads, II. 155.
Sheep, Buying, I. 55; of Ili, 71.
Shepherds, Thibetan, II. 4, 94.
Shèr Agha, I. 97.
Shisougoune River, II. 194.
Siberia, I. 39.
Sibos, I. 9.
Sickness, Desert, I. 131.
Sickness, Mountain, I. 141, 142, 143, 166, 183.
Silos, II. 23.
Sinin-Fou, I. 159; II. 79, 154, 211.
Sling, Skill of Thibetans with the, II. 102.
Smallpox in the region of the Tchershène, I. 74, 100.
Snipe, II. 144.
Snow on the mountains, I. 12, 23; on Ningling Tangla, II. 33; relieving headache, 116.
Snuff-box of a Thibetan, II. 2.
Snuff-taking, by natives of Arkan, I. 70; by ambassadors from Lhassa, II. 45.
So, II. 93, 103; lama-house at, 105; singular construction of the houses at, 106; palace at, 106.
Soap, Sap of *tougrak* trees used as, I. 67.
Sokpon, The, their massacre of Thibetans, II. 165.
Solitude of the desert, I. 24.
Solons, I. 9.
Songs, Native, I. 97, 118, 132; II. 135.
Sostchou River, II. 100, 112.
Soubrou, II. 77.
Soudjou, Valley of, II. 115.
Sougomba, Bridge of, II. 154.
Sounds, Peculiar, in high altitudes, I. 202.
Souti, II. 115.
Sparrows, II. 27, 144.
Spinning-wheel of a Thibetan, II. 3.
Spring of Archan Buluk, I. 35.
Springs, Hot, I. 205, 211, 217; II. 35, 159.
St. Denys, Marquis d'Hervey de, I. 48.

INDEX.

Stags, I. 212.
Stags at Bougou Bashi, I. 72.
Storm in the defile of Kalchigué-gol, I. 32.
Sugar, its effect on the Thibetans, II. 11, 18.
Swallows, I. 88, 117.
Swans, Wild, I. 88, 107.
Syringas, II. 194.

Ta-Amban, The, II. 56-62, 71-73, 84-87.
Ta-Lama, The, II. 56-62, 71-73, 84-87.
Talai-Lama, The, II. 3, 8, 11, 37, 80, 147.
Talkitchin, I. 71; salt at, 71.
Tamarisks, I. 12, 38, 62, 68, 71, 108, 131.
Tambourine accompaniment to prayers, I. 19; II. 132.
Tandi, II. 101.
Tarantshis, The, I. 7, 8; their abandonment of wives, 9; at Kourla, 42.
Tarim River, The, I. 62, 63, 65; overflow of, 65; action of the wind upon the sands of, 67; *tchiga* plants in the valley of, 68; salt on the banks of, 69; breadth of, 79, 90; and the "Lake" of Lob Nor, 90, 109; the travellers' descent of, 92; ice in, 106.
Taro, II. 172.
Tartars, The, and their horses, I. 61.
Tash-Dawan Mountain, I. 134, 140; crossing the, 141; 217.
Tashé-Roua, II. 74.
Tashiline, II. 135.
Tashkend, I. 7.
Tatchou River, II. 143.
Tatsien-Lou, II. 74, 133, 134, 167, 196, 204; treatment of the travellers at, 209; 210.
Taxes levied by Chinese, I. 67, 89, 164.
Tchaï, I. 107.
Tchamdo, *see* Tsiamdo.
Tchang (fermented barley), II. 199.
Tcharkal, *see* Tcharkalik.
Tcharkalik, I. 74, 99, 111; "French party" erected at, 115.
Tchershène Darya River, I. 72.
Tcherchène, I. 164.
Tchiga plants, I. 68; woven into garments, 68; 71.
Tchigali, *Tchiga* plants at, I. 68.
Tchimbo-Nara, II. 136.
Tchimbo-Tinzi, II. 136.
Tchimène Tagh, The, I. 113, 149.
Tchimène, Plateau of, I. 150.
Tchinagi, I. 57; origin of inhabitants, and their customs, 58, 59.
Tchoukour Saï, I. 133.
Tchoungo, II. 143.
Tchounneu, II. 173.
Tchoupalongue, II. 201.
Tchouzma, A dish of, I. 197.
Tea, the favourite drink of the Mongols and the Thibetans, I. 16; trade between China and Thibet in, II. 188.
Tengri Nor (the Namtso), II. 32.
Tent of the Amban of Lhassa, II. 50.
Tents of Thibetans, II. 23, 113, 172.

Terai, Tint of sky at, I. 76.
Terek-Dawan, The, I. 41.
Thibet Higher table-lands of, I. 2; difficulties of travelling in, 7; tea-drinking in, 16; intermixture of the people with the Lobis, 133; pasture-ground of, 217; the first native encountered by the travellers, II. 2; ruins of dwellings in, 131; electric phenomenon from woollen garments in, 114; general appearance of the mountains, 144; fine scenery near Djala Mountains, 147; iron manufactory at Lagoum, 150; no trustworthy history, 165; tea trade with China, 188; weakness of Chinese authority in, 191.
Thibetans: the first native met by the travellers, II. 2; their snuff-taking, 2; native deception, 3; a shepherd and a shepherdess, 4, 5; their greediness, 5; their ponies, 5; their wonder at English revolvers, 6; their pigtails, 8; large tongues, 11, 12; meat-venders, 17; tents, 23; mills and saddles, 23; of Lhassa, 37-40; loading yaks, 64; cooking, 76; their characteristics near Lhassa, 78, 79; armed horsemen, 80; yak-drivers, 83, 98; exchange of presents with the chiefs from Lhassa, 84, 86; shepherds, 94, 114; their dogs, 96; variety of types, 96, 97, 99, 115, 163; signs with the thumbs, 98, 111, 118, 150; modes of salutation, 2, 8, 18, 48, 98; forms of religion, 99; their skill with the sling, 102; houses and people of So, 105-112; coins, 108; huts, 114; tobacco-smoking, 114; extortions of chiefs, 116; goitres, 116; fine specimen of a chief, 122; flat houses, 121; polyandry and polygamy, 124-127; tasks laid upon women, 127; a drunken chief, 136; a domestic scene, 139; vacillation, 140; superstition, 140; agricultural implements, 143; care for cattle, 143; veneration for the pagoda at Djala Pass, 147; their kindness of heart contrasted with the unfeeling nature of the Chinese, 164, 165; their insolence at Lendjoune, 166; a fight about a yak-skin, 170; superstitions, 183, 191.
Thomine, Father, II. 195.
Thrushes, I. 35.
Thumb, Signing a treaty with the, I. 124.
Thumbs, Signs with the, II. 98, 111, 118, 150.
Tien Shan, The, I. 7, 10, 19; Buddhist inscriptions on the slopes of, 31.
Tientsin Treaty, The, II. 203.
Tigers, I. 67, 82.
Timour, shepherd and servant to the travellers, I. 113, 123, 149, 156; searches for lost horses, 181; at the burial of Niaz, 193; II. 90.
Timurlik, I. 19, 152.
Tiskène, Plains of, I. 174.
Tiumen, I. 3, 121.
Tjéma-Loung, II. 102.
Tobolsk, I. 58.

Tokta, a village singer, I. 118, 119; playing the *allah-rabôb*, 132, 145; 170.
Tomtits, I. 35.
Tonquin, Route from Paris to, I. 2; 7, 111; reception of the travellers at, II. 219.
Tools used in an iron manufactory, II. 151.
Torgots, The, I. 27, 30, 32; their descent, 35; 36; photographed by Prince Henry, 38; 39, 151.
Tougrak, Woods of, I. 62; sap of, used as soap, 67.
Touin Kwiruk, I. 38.
Tsaïdam, The, I. 6, 111, 116, 155; II. 77.
Transmigration of the soul, I. 14, 30; II. 99.
Tsakma, Valley of the, I. 19, 23.
Tsatang, II. 95.
Tsiamdo, II. 105, 118, 149, 167, 195.
Tsong Kaba, I. 31; II. 80.
Tsong li Yamen, The, at Pekin, I. 6.
Tsonké, II. 173.
Tson-ron River, II. 173.
Tumblers, Thibetan, II. 135.
Turfan, I. 89.
Turkestan, Chinese, I. 2.
Turkestan, Russian, I. 4, 52.
Turks, Fine specimens of, I. 3.
Turnip, or *niomna*, II. 115, 143.

Ugliness of Thibetans, II. 2, 6.
Ulcers, I. 100.
Urumtsi, Highway of, I. 120.
Unicorn, Reputed existence of the, II. 68.
Ural Mountains, I. 3.
Uzbegs, The, I. 3, 40.

Valley of bones, A, I. 206.
Valleys of China, I. 2.
Vase made from a yak's skull, II. 23.
Violets, II. 155.
Volcanoes, The Reclus, I. 187, 188; the Ruysbruk, or Rubruquis, 194, 198; cones of several, 198.
Volga, The, I. 3, 35.
Vultures, II. 35.

Wagner, M., French Consul at Shanghai, II. 211.
Wagtails, I. 35.

Water-carriers, II. 77, 78.
Water-mill, A Thibetan, II. 191.
Water-fowl, I. 68, 83, 88.
"Waves of mountains," I. 204.
Wells from the Aryk, I. 118.
Wheat at Aktarma, I. 65.
Wild Camels, I. 82, 87.
Wilderness of mountains, A, I. 198–218.
Willows, I. 12, 20, 38; II. 155.
Windmills, Praying, II. 143.
Wives, Abandonment of, by Mussulmans, I. 9.
Wolves, I. 25, 67, 135, 188, 199, 210; II. 31, 93, 101, 163.
Women; their ugliness amongst the Mongols, I. 19; II. 24, 28; at Kourla, I. 52; of Abdallah, 84, 105; amongst shepherd tribes, II. 94; smearing their faces with butter, 96, 117; assisting in building, 112; filthiness of, 117; ornaments of, 124, 139; as beggars, 126; laborious life of, 127, 133; as field labourers, 141, 164; as yak-drivers, 160; near Taro, 173; dancing near Batang, 199, 200.

Yakoob-Beg, the "blessed one," I. 40; poisoned at Kourla, 41: 57, 58, 61; fortress constructed by, 72.
Yaks, I. 149, 166, 175, 194; enormous specimens of, 200; 205; an ancient specimen, 206; 212, 215; II. 8, 47, 94; breaking through the ice, 95; 101; falling over a precipice, 103; in inaccessible places, 116.
Yandachkak, I. 131.
Yang-tse-Kiang, Probable sources of, I. 208; II. 194, 195.
Yangi Koul, I. 65; characteristics of the inhabitants of, 66.
Yantag, I. 36, 38.
"Yourt," Remains of a Thibetan, I. 210.
Youtchap Khan, Characteristics of the inhabitants of, I. 91.
Yulduz, The, I. 20, 28, 30.
Yunnan, II. 123, 196, 212.

Zakisto-gol, The, I. 30.
Zamba, II. 26, 41.
Zetchou River, II. 152.

www.ingramcontent.com/pod-product-compliance
Lightning Source LLC
Chambersburg PA
CBHW021805230426
43669CB00008B/641